CHALLENGES
TO AMERICAN VALUES

CHALLENGES
TO AMERICAN VALUES
SOCIETY, BUSINESS, AND RELIGION

THOMAS C. COCHRAN

OXFORD UNIVERSITY PRESS
New York   Oxford

Oxford University Press

Oxford   New York   Toronto
Delhi   Bombay   Calcutta   Madras   Karachi
Petaling Jaya   Singapore   Hong Kong   Tokyo
Nairobi   Dar es Salaam   Cape Town
Melbourne   Auckland

and associated companies in
Beirut   Berlin   Ibadan   Nicosia

First published in 1985 by Oxford University Press, Inc.
200 Madison Avenue, New York, New York 10016
First issued as an Oxford University Press paperback, 1986

Oxford is a registered trademark of Oxford University Press

Library of Congress Cataloging in Publication Data
Cochran, Thomas Childs, 1902–
Challenges to American values.
1. United States—Economic conditions.   2. United
States—Social conditions.   3. Industry—Social aspects—
United States—History.   4. Social values.   I. Title.
HC103.C623   1985   306'.0973   84-19102
ISBN 0-19-503534-8 (cloth)
ISBN 0-19-503535-6 (paper)

2 4 6 8 10 9 7 5 3 1
Printed in the United States of America

To Anne M. Witmer,
whose upbringing in European culture
and training in American studies
have been a constant help.

Preface

The ideas in this essay essentially form the basis of an effort to use knowledge based on historical development. Coming from a lifetime of study of American history, the values discussed may stimulate readers to further thought and deeper understanding.

The chapters are not narrative history, but rather brief summaries of long periods of value formation or challenge. Agreement with the statements presented is not necessary; my aim is to suggest that historical progress presents new problems and that some deeply rooted American values have not always offered the best basis for meeting or solving such difficulties. Put another way, adequately understanding the origins and ramifications of an apparent dilemma may put one on a path toward its solution. I hope to suggest some new questions, which may evoke new answers.

Radnor, Pa.   T. C. C.
August, 1984

Contents

PART I

THE HERITAGE
OF VALUES
1607-1850

1

History and Values

A practical man of long and wide experience in American affairs has written of the current "centerless, disaffected, alienated, uncommitted and disappointed society." His alarming view is not based on any single failure but on what he sees as a general breakdown in commonly held values.[1] Though many may judge Mandel's pessimism to be extreme, similar ideas have been widespread among commentators on the latest decades of the twentieth century. Further understanding of the nature of these deep disaffections may be gained by tracing the origins and evolution of the challenges to deeply entrenched American values.

I have selected values as the area of conflict between novelty and tradition because they are regarded by social scientists as a "specially economical set of high level guidance signals."[2] The conflicts have also been little explored from long-run historical evidence.[3] At the highest levels of generalization, which will of necessity dominate this brief discussion, values and norms of social behavior tend to merge. Consequently, the discussion becomes one of challenges to customary American views and behavior.

Many of the challenged values were imported from Europe and are older than the nation. In the first two centuries of settlement, Americans altered the European heritage to fit the new environment and developed a widely held set of social or cultural values. Although there were numerous differences in local customs, varying from those of a South Carolina planter to those of a Maine fisherman or from those of the Reverend Cotton Mather of Boston to those of the merchant Simon Gratz of Philadelphia, there were also common elements in American ideas and attitudes quickly recognized by visitors from other countries. These distinguished and learned travelers described the similarities somewhat differently, but from the early commentators to Francis Grund and Alexis de Tocqueville in the 1830s, they agreed on many distinctive American characteristics.

Similarities in values and general culture from North to South were partly the result of common foreign backgrounds as well as of sharing the experience of migration and settlement. Except for black slaves, early settlers came from northwestern Europe; and they all had to adjust to living on the edge of a wilderness where life was originally simple and rigorous. The common cultural values that were generated by these circumstances persisted in spite of later migrations and economic and social changes. Among the attributes that were valued more than, or differently from, those in Europe were individual initiative and responsibility, self-determination, private rights, material success, belief in an immanent God, and impatience with apparently nonutilitarian activities or learning, and white male supremacy. Obviously, this list of traditional values could be made longer without encountering much disagreement. These attitudes bred in the colonies were well suited to the development of the United States up to the mid-nineteenth century, but from that time on the old beliefs have been challenged by physical and psychological changes stemming from technology and new social needs that resulted by 1980 in a society strained by conflicting values and a new environment.

Culture and Society

For theoretical purposes, social scientists divide society into culture, social institutions, and physical environment. Cul-

ture embraces all that people think and do, but it is not necessary to explore all aspects of culture in order to assess the
force of its historically important social values.[4] The sharing
of a number of values such as those placed on individualism,
equality before the law, or the virtue of material success
makes for a harmonious society, while challenges to a sufficient number of basic values is deeply disturbing. Social institutions are customary ways of doing things, and culture includes the meanings we attach to such activities. Social
structure is made up of institutions, some represented in
stone and mortar as in churches, others in patterns of action
such as electing government officials.[5] In their actions as
members of the society, people who do not outwardly follow
the values and support the institutions of their culture are
regarded as innovators or deviants.[6]

The admonitions given by parents to their children maintain continuity in culture and values. In early America these
included indoctrination with many traditional European
values plus instructions on how to get along under the new
conditions. Playmates and schooling added to parental influences, but before 1800 formal learning for most young
children came at home. Later in life came the additional
values, norms, admonitions, or ideas picked up at work, in
church, at social gatherings, or by the written word, though
presumably there was not much of the latter, for even most
of the literate read with some difficulty.

Scholars in many fields have felt increasingly the need for
some more precise understanding of how cultural components such as values, beliefs, desires, habits, and norms actually operate. In the course of this quest, analysts have been
forced to recognize that actions speak louder than words,
that the influence of cultural values in the history of nations
such as the United States should be interpreted more on the
basis of what was done than on how it was verbally justified.
The colonists, for example, rebelled against controls from
abroad for local, social, and economic reasons, but a few
lawyers or philosophers justified their actions by natural law

and the unwritten English constitution. Or to put it another way, Americans as a people have tended to be nonintellectual; hence efforts to interpret their history on the basis of formally expressed ideas often appear superficial and misleading.

Because values are shaped necessarily from past experiences, the existing culture is a conservative rather than a dynamic social force. Changes usually come first in the social environment in which persons play their roles. Clearly, some cultures, such as that of an entrenched aristocracy, have more ability to resist change than that of a migratory democracy. A type of change that is hard to resist is one stemming from gradual, cumulative processes such as the growth in density of population, slow exhaustion of soil or minerals, or the growth of bureaucracies. Such forces bring gradual adjustments in roles and values that people are unaware of except by careful comparisons with earlier times.

Migration, Geography, and Values

Migration to a new type of environment, whether the country or a city, is a major force for innovation and cultural modification. The size of such continuous movement has made America an exceptional case in recent world history.[7] There had, of course, been massive migrations in an early period in Europe and Asia, and everywhere there had been a certain amount of work-oriented movement by artisans and laborers, but not in recent centuries had there been continuous resettlement of a high percentage of the total population. For most colonists who came to America, the ocean trip was merely a first move. As the population grew, families continually sold old land and moved to new land, or, if they remained artisans, they moved from the ports of debarkation to newer cities or towns. Most people repeated the process more than once in a lifetime, becoming used to entering a cultural environment in which geography and artifacts might be relatively familiar, but their neighbors were strangers.

Confrontation with the new, whether on a frontier or in a metropolitan area, had certain uniform repercussions. Movers brought relatively few household goods with them and wanted new supplies at a low cost. The average new-comers were not in a position to haggle about artistic designs or fine finishes; utility was their overriding need. In addition, wise families looking forward to further migration continued to stock their homes, farms, or shops on the same basis. "You can't take it with you" was more than a popular religious aphorism. No matter how short the move, adjustment to a new environment stimulated innovations, large or small. Friends had to be made easily and easily given up when one or the other party left. Practically all the values attributed by Turner to the "frontier" were generated by the process of continuing migration, as well as some that Turner would not have celebrated.[8] While a degree of social democracy developed from the migration of nuclear families unsupported by wealthy collateral relatives, often this was not completely the case. In a Wisconsin county studied by Merle E. Curti, the original leaders, businessmen who started the settlement, perpetuated their strong influence in politics for a generation.[9] Yet in all places growing from rapid migration there undoubtedly was an easier going, less formal attitude, a necessary combining of cooperation with individual initiative, and a neighborliness in excess of that in the older East Coast areas of out-migration.

In a broad sense most social sanctions lost some of their force in a migratory population. Yet religious values and beliefs were undoubtedly strengthened in the Colonial period by the belief of many people that this was the biblical promised land, God's New World. Religious values may not have been more widespread in Colonial culture than in Europe, but, among large parts of the population, they appear to have been a stronger force for social action.

The common sets of cultural "policies" and values that gradually grew to meet recurring situations in all parts of America will appear in connection with later challenges and responses. Migration has continued to be a powerful influence throughout American history. In the decade 1920 to 1930, for example, an old stable East Coast city such as Norristown, Pennsylvania, received 501 new male migrants and lost 382. For the whole period 1910 to 1950, in-migration accounted for 80 percent of the growth in male population.[10]

Geography also led to modifications of the values of European cultures. Abundance of fertile land was not only responsible for internal migration but also for innovations in the practices of farmers, shopkeepers and millers that, in turn, changed the culture. American farming, for example, was carried on in a strikingly different environment in soils, living conditions, and climates from those in Great Britain or continental Europe. Migration and cheap land tended to make all adult males, urban or rural, into real estate operators.

Navigable rivers flowing into the frequent and large bays from Cape Hatteras northward were also a powerful influence toward business activity that inevitably influenced agrarian values. Farmers in New York State nearly two hundred miles inland, if near the Mohawk River, could float goods downstream in the spring flood waters for sale in urban markets. Small sailboats and pole boats made their way up and down shallow rivers during periods of high water with flour, wood, iron, and other inland products that would come first to the seaports and eventually go to Europe or the West Indies. But well before the American Revolution, major customers were the growing American towns and cities. Iron, lying on the surface of the ground in some areas from Virginia to New England, made this staple of modern society readily available in surplus quantities. Wood was so plentiful that most trees were regarded as hindrances rather than assets.

These opportunities of the American geographical environment support the thesis that such forces working on the continuous flow of immigrants with the lower- to middle-class Western European cultural heritage were dominant in shaping the traditional American values and social practices. The total approach, therefore, may be called "geocultural." The physical environment was exploited by people with the cultural values and knowledge needed for material success, and, in doing so, they generated a common culture and values that for many decades became stronger as well as more distinct from those of Europe.

Values and Later Challenges

American culture has continued to stress strongly such traits as optimism, to value utility highly, and to be preoccupied with physical things and their improvement. The fact that great value was placed on religion by influential groups in the population did not seem to be at odds with an optimistic materialism. If modifications were made, as in the case of Puritanical Calvinism, it was the theology that was modified, chiefly in weakening the anxiety about predestination, rather than in changing the practical attitudes of the believers. In all, the benefits of the American environment seem to have gone well with an optimistic and locally varied belief in God's grace and its manifestation.

Thus Europeans exposed to the influence of America developed enduring and unique cultural values. From the eighteenth century on, new material forces such as the development of power machinery impinged on traditional values, but for more than a century the existing culture was highly congenial to the then current physical changes. The pursuit of personal success, commitment to material progress, placing a high value on activity as such, individual—not social—responsibility, and other norms of the democratic, individualistic, and historic capitalist values were all reenforced rather than undermined in the first generations of an industrializing society.

By the mid-nineteenth century the relative maturity of American industry and the sudden emergence of a nation of continental size from the Mexican War, one tied together by rail and telegraph, posed new physical problems. For meeting these conditions, the values of the old culture were no longer ideally suited. The social planning forced by big urban centers, the large bureaucracies needed by both business and government in order to operate on a continental scale, the devotion to scientific research required to advance increasingly intricate and theoretical technology, and the recognition of social as well as individual causes for failure and hardship all challenged the old core of cultural values.

2

The Colonial Heritage

Of early nineteenth century America, de Tocqueville wrote: "We shall remain perfectly convinced that not an opinion, not a custom, not a law, I may even say not an event, is upon record which the origin of that people won't explain."[1] Put another way, up to that time the changes in inherited values and norms had tended to reenforce rather than challenge colonial patterns. And since many of the essentials of this early environment continued long after the Colonial Period, a large part of the early cultural adjustments were reenacted on the frontiers of later times.

Uniformities Among Settlers

The early migrants to the Southern coastline expected to become farmers or planters, and, except for the enslaved blacks, they were predominantly British. In the Middle Colonies some of the pioneers were Dutch and Swedish but surrounded by others from the British Isles. Later on, William Penn brought not only English Quakers but also large numbers of German sectarians. French Huguenots, dissenters from the established Catholic Church, also settled in several places in the Middle States. Although the earliest New Englanders were English, latecomers were also Scotch, Irish and Scotch-Irish, often moving after a few years on to the backcountry of the colonies to the West and South.

All these early immigrants on the Atlantic coast between Georgia and Maine came from the group of nations that already led the world in the building of water mills, metal processing, and mechanical devices ranging from clocks to public works. Almost every eighteenth-century boatload of settlers had artisans among them familiar with some aspect of advanced technology. There was, however, a kind of technological imbalance in all of these nations of continental Europe. Skilled technicians could have improved complex machinery for power, drilling, or shaping, for which Europe offered an inadequate market. Thus, technology had a potential in excess of effective demand. In America, however, there was an urgent need for new practical devices. The artisan who might have made a complicated automaton for fairs or exhibitions in Europe designed a better pump, stove, or wagon in America. As Siegfried Gideon wrote, "Imagination was given scope to shape reality unhindered."[2]

But the flow of skilled artisans, though differing from the settlers going to Portuguese or Spanish colonies, should not be overemphasized. The majority of settlers were farmers, unskilled workers, and prisoners, all seeking escape from an unpleasant life. The indenture system allowing immigrants to gain passage in return for selling their labor for several years was probably the most frequent means of financing white migration to the colonies.

Without regard to the particular characteristics of these European settlers or of the new environment, Americans were necessarily affected by the characteristics of any area growing from migration. The newcomers were continually forced to modify previously conditioned patterns of action to fit different situations; "experience was not a series of familiar events, but an unfolding scene of exploration."[3] Thrown with strangers, the migrant was not sure what their responses would be to his or her customary behavior. Migrants usually shared unfamiliar or unknown social status. As noted earlier, the traits that Frederick Jackson Turner attributed to the frontier such as democracy, self-reliance, practicality, and acceptance of new habits were those ascribed by demographers to all areas of rapid in-migration.

Regardless of how or why they came, most of the white migrants to North America shared certain characteristics. They were willing to risk about a two-month ocean voyage, during which or from the effects of which many would die. Many were relative misfits in their own countries because of unorthodox religion, economic obstacles to careers, or strong ambition to get ahead. In 1685, for example, the revocation of the Edict of Nantes that had granted toleration to French Protestants (Huguenots) led to an outflow of many unusually able artisans and farmers who established settlements in several parts of the British colonies. From all of Western Europe skilled craftsmen were stimulated to move by the hereditary and restrictive policies of the artisan guilds in the major cities, which denied many ambitious men the hope of a secure place in society. In fact, so strong was the incentive to try the New World that in some decades of the mid-eighteenth century there was a surplus of skilled artisans in the northern Colonial ports of debarkation. Eventually, these men and their descendants took their skills to the interior cities such as Hartford, Kingston, or Lancaster.

The majority of the colonists, however, after gaining their freedom if indentured or immediately free in the case of planned colonies such as parts of Pennsylvania, became moderately self-sufficient farmers. The newcomers naturally sought to preserve the particular culture they had brought with them. On the backcountry farms, where a majority of the population lived, early Colonial society was still conservative and traditional.[4] But in the mid-eighteenth century increases in the population of Europe and the West Indies began to raise the price of grains and other food products that American farms could supply. The result was a gradual drawing of more and more farmers into producing for a commercial market and hence into having an interest in better transportation and increasing productivity.

This trend continued far beyond the Colonial period and, together with other factors such as large acreages and migration, hindered the perpetuation of the conservative European type of village and family farm culture. Farmer George Washington wrote in 1784: "The spirit for trade which pervades these states is not to be restrained."[5]

Colonial Uniformities

United on the practical side by much common training and many similar aims, the colonists had more uniform religious beliefs than would be supposed from the variety of their sects. Winthrop S. Hudson writes: "At the beginning American society was largely homogeneous sharing common assumptions and common patterns of behavior. Ethnic and religious diversity was modest. The major diversity was ecclesiastical—a variety of forms within the context of a common religious faith."[6] It has been said that Britain exported its religious pattern to the colonies, including the factions that had executed Charles I. But there was an important difference. In the colonies the Anglicans or Episcopalians were a small minority with little government support outside of Virginia. The dissident sects, including those of French, Dutch, and German origins, were chiefly offshoots of Calvinism with only slight variations in biblical interpretation dividing them, as were the Scotch Presbyterians. It is said that by the eighteenth century Connecticut Presbyterians were closer in belief to the original English Puritans than were the latters' direct descendants, the Congregationalists of Massachusetts.

In the mid-eighteenth century the various Protestant faiths responded to the preaching of George Whitefield, Jonathan Edwards, and other evangelists to produce a burst of religious enthusiasm called the Great Awakening. The "rebirth" experienced by those who saw the light made their religion more personal and less social. For this reason the "New Light" evangelicals were less interested in resistance to Great Britain than were the "Old Light" sect.[7] Except for a small number of Catholics, and an even smaller number of Jews, however, the pre-Revolutionary churches had evangelical, Bible-centered beliefs that differed more in forms than basic theology. So much was this true throughout the first three centuries of American culture that one may speak of the civic or public religion of the United States with its belief in God as revealed through Christ and the Testaments. In this sense, the ministers who passed on the news and politics of the day to people who would not, or could not, read a six-cent newspaper, did much to perpetuate values and form public opinion.

There was little, if any, contradiction between strong religious belief and American utilitarianism or striving for material success. In fact, quite the opposite. The regular churchgoer(s) were, on the whole, successful, and those who had not succeeded were likely to lack such strong belief or, in the words of Governor Dongan of New York in 1687, to have "none at all."[8]

One should not form an idealized picture of the colonial immigrants or their new society. Between 1720 and 1770 about half of the Scotch living in Northern Ireland came to America. They brought their own cultural patterns that altered only slowly. Many were bigoted Presbyterians, made combative and aggressive by their quarrels with Catholics and the British government in Ulster. Though most colonists, regardless of sex or origin, drank heavily by today's standards, the Scotch-Irish built a reputation for excesses. And while the Puritans of the Bay Colony were among the most orderly and the most interested in education, their rigorousness in both learning and theology declined as time went on. By the eighteenth century, the Puritan areas of Connecticut and

Massachusetts were becoming less committed to religion and education and more interested in trade. Many of the newcomers to all the colonies could not read or write and passed illiteracy on to their children. Thus, the illiterate, indigent, urban poor became an increasing colonial problem. Ministers devoted sermons to diligence in business or the dangers of debt.[9] On the farms, which accounted for over 90 percent of the population, there was always the possibility of improvement from harder work or better methods. The Calvinist-based religions (Congregational, Presbyterian, Baptist, Quaker, and minor sects) all justified work and devotion to one's calling, not contemplative or scholarly withdrawal from the world.

Perhaps the most important difference from all of Northern and Western Europe in the physical surroundings of the newcomers was an unwanted surplus of wood. The Indians, few in number, had done only a minimal amount of farming. Consequently, most of the land was covered by forests with many great hardwood trees, some of more than three feet in diameter. Any colonist who felled a tree was regarded as a public benefactor. Removing stumps was far too laborious, and crops were planted between them. The immediate effect was to confine the bounds of settlement; the long-run effects were to build the world's most mechanized woodworking industry and strengthen the cultural trait of putting a low value on raw materials and a high value on labor.

From their surface deposits of iron, the colonies from Virginia on north produced by 1770 more pig iron than England and Wales combined. In order to ensure a supply of pig iron to the forges of Britain and encourage British exports of finished ironware in return, a regulation of 1734 forbade new iron or steel processing plants in the colonies. In spite of British laws, however, American artisans continued to expand ironworking. Families also spun wool and flax and made cloth at home. Thus the northern colonies supplied their everyday needs for manufactures and, in general, imported only luxury or special goods from abroad. Benjamin Franklin boasted, "I do not know a single imported article into the northern colonies but what they can either do without or make themselves."[10]

In contrast, the Southern colonies sent their tobacco, rice, and indigo directly to Great Britain and hence found it convenient to do their buying there. As a result, Great Britain valued the Southern colonies and regarded the Northern ones as potential rivals of home industry. Thus, though in comparison to the period after the American Revolution the Colonial era seems static, in fact, it was one with an economically developing society whose rates of change and innovation, somewhat retarded by British regulations, were still about as rapid as those of northwestern Europe. In spite of some urban poverty, the general standard of living by 1770 was perhaps the highest in the world.[11]

Government and Values

By European standards the colonists were uniquely conditioned in their attitudes toward government. The earliest English settlements, Jamestown and Plymouth, were not imperialist ventures by the British Crown; they were financed as profit-seeking enterprises largely by London merchants. With the financial failure of both the London and Virginia companies, a large measure of self-government was granted royally to the settlers. In the later case of Massachusetts Bay, the company and its Puritan financial backers moved to America and continued until 1684 to be governed under their corporate charter. Later ventures such as those of Lord Baltimore or William Penn were initiated by large royal grants of land to proprietors that included limited rights to govern.

In all cases, both the Crown and the proprietors found it expedient to delegate local political powers to substantial property owners. Hence without ringing phrases such as "all men are created equal" or "freedom and democracy" or much acquaintance with the writings of John Locke, the culture led substantial citizens to expect to control local government and gave them experience with representative processes. Colonial political culture, that is, was not truly democratic in either thought or action, but it trained citizens in the processes needed for a democratic government.

Another aspect of Colonial government that was to leave a lasting mark on the American cultural heritage was lack of a locally controlled civil or military bureaucracy. In the mature form of Colonial administration, governors were generally appointed by Britain and were usually Englishmen. Their supporting officers were almost always colonials, but were few in numbers and appointed by the governor. In peacetime, military commanders and troops were British, as were customs collectors and some minor officials. The effect of this lack of control of either military or civil bureaucracy by local authorities was to close such careers to most of the sons of the wealthy and to foster a view of the central imperial government as a potential adversary. Even the Episcopal Church, established in New York, New Jersey, and the Southern colonies, had no local bishops. Hence in this topless Colonial society the roads to prestige were essentially in land, including urban real estate, or trade. And because wealth from land meant producing for the market, one may generalize that business, not government, was the road to Colonial success. This also led to a lack of prestige attached to government careers and to high respect for those in business that became enduring values in American culture.[12]

The Heritage

To say that the "spirit of capitalism" had triumphed by the end of the Colonial period is not as exact as saying that the value placed on both utility and financial success was generally higher than in other cultures. The inevitable mixing of faiths from new migrants and the pursuit of material success shaped religious doctrines even in New England. The process of assimilating businesslike values was probably even faster in the more prosperous Middle Colonies. In Philadelphia, children's paddles, home teaching devices, typically illustrated the alphabet in the seventeenth century by phrases such as "*A* is for Adam in whose fall we sinned all"; by the eighteenth century, typical phrases were "*A* is for Almanac, will you buy an Almanac"; "*B* Buy a Broom."[13]

Only small communities, such as those of the Pennsylvania Amish or Mennonites, preserved their religious intensity in the face of secular development. In the quest for material success, people might justify complete commitment to business as doing God's work. Practically they did not have to protect freedom of religion or democracy; they needed to and did protect legal equality or opportunity under changing conditions. A faculty-student seminar, financed by the Ford Foundation at the University of Pennsylvania, spent much of one term on searching for the historical meaning of "individualism" in America. The bulk of the evidence indicated that it meant protection of individual equality and property rights. De Tocqueville had come to much the same conclusion. In contrast to some European cultures, American individualism included placing a high value on the ease of cooperation in handling large timbers for houses, barns, mills, or stores; people readily came together for such purposes and hence for other community needs. The cultural place of the church and of private voluntary associations for many purposes, so noted by European commentators, stretches back to this early and continuing type of cooperation.

In spite of strongly developed cultural traits of easy innovation or adjustment to change, individual initiative, ready cooperation, and a general belief in God and equality before the law, Colonial values had their less attractive sides. America was a dynamic society in which failure was frequent and was not condoned. In the 1760s, 60 percent of Boston's municipal revenue went for a miserable level of poor relief.[14] The situation was little better in the more prosperous Colonial city of Philadelphia, where a tenth of the population were estimated to be impoverished.[15] The admiration for activity as such carried with it an impatience with thought and a disdain for scholarly contemplation. Among the middle to lower classes, reading, if done at all, was often done secretly. The weakening of the disciplines or values imposed by European social structures led to unreliability in conduct; and ease of migration away from one's creditors increased dishonesty. As writers from Europe were to observe for a century, American culture and its society were relatively vigorous, religious, aspiring, progressive, and democratic, but also lacking in erudition, unreliable in conduct, crude in manners, and wasteful of materials. Until almost the twentieth century the differences seemed no hindrance to America as a nation. The challenges of more recent years are forcing reconsideration.

3

Old Values Reenforced

From 1775 on, both the course of events and the progress of technology gave new strength to the values of the activist, utilitarian, individualistic, and democratic American culture. Never has a nation been faced with more exciting possibilities than the new United States. Citizens confidently expected great and beneficent changes resulting from the first large society growing under conditions new to the history of the world. Americans enjoyed a representative government, free male equality before the law, versatile artisans unhindered by guilds or traditions, citizens striving for individual success, seemingly limitless farmland, and widespread belief in a mandate from God to produce His "New World" before the Second Coming.

In this new society formed by adventurous immigrants from highly civilized nations of the Old World, the urges of the aesthetic sense tended to take the courses of technological creation and nature worship. Possessing inherited skills and motivated by drives for self-fulfillment, artisan copiers and innovators produced within two generations an explosion in technology that was to make the United States the world leader in mass production. Meanwhile, conservative statesmen created a federal structure that did not violate too strongly the provincial loyalties built up over more than a century, one that left the states free to aid local or regional development, as they would have done earlier if permitted to do so by Great Britain. Religious values, temporarily superseded by the upsets of war, returned to their former strength after 1800 and made the United States the foremost nation in belief in God's immanence.

That the basic traits of the culture were more reenforced than altered by the American Revolution and the formation of new governments strikingly illustrates the receptiveness of the old and deeply held values to the new conditions as well as the continuing influence of geography and migration. In addition, existing values were highly favorable for the technological changes that rapidly took place. Aside from the growing problem of slavery, the inherited norms and values prepared citizens to take advantage of the immediate possibilities of the new nation. As compared to Europe, America never had to "modernize." An older way of life did not have to be abandoned, and no deeply ingrained hereditary institutions had to be altered significantly or destroyed. Existing cultural values were congenial to the new ways, and older norms rapidly incorporated the small changes necessary. The new industrial mills, for example, were largely in the countryside; and the workers, in general, mixed farming, factory work, and other occupations into their traditionally migratory lives.

Obviously, the cultural values involved in the new politics, religion, and technology had differing relations to social change. Overall, religion was an essentially conservative social force seeking to maintain the beliefs and values of the seventeenth century. Meanwhile, politics was for the most part formalizing practices based on ideas stemming from the Revolution and the experiences of Colonial status. The problems of various sectional interests under federalism were met with some reluctance and, as the Civil War was to show, never resolved into common cultural values. Technological development, though tending to be free of ideology or social intent, nevertheless changed the realities of work, home life, and geographical relations in ways that forced minor but continuing adjustments in values and norms. Those writing about the coming of industrialism to the United States, however, have generally exaggerated the impact of these changes.

Technology and Values

Recent studies indicate that the values of the common people in France as well as in Great Britain were favorable to improvements in physical devices, but in these European nations there was opposition from powerful groups who might be adversely affected by change. In contrast, in the northeastern United States all classes united in an interest in physical progress. Another advantage of this part of the United States was that wood and water for power were abundant, and this freed America from Great Britain's costly reliance on coal and steam. Compensating for this American leadership in resources and favorable values were higher levels of technical knowledge in both Great Britain and France. But because the technology of the eighteenth century was relatively simple and skilled immigrants continually came to the United States, lack of exact European knowledge was a small obstacle easily overcome. The physical endowment of the East Coast from Virginia on north was so favorable to industrial progress that had Great Britain not legally discouraged or forbidden incorporation, improved inland transportation, banking, and some finished manufactures, American technological progress might have been rapid from 1750 on, and the period from 1783 to 1820 would have seemed less revolutionary.

Industrialization and the resulting creation of "modern" society have taken unique forms in every nation. Even small European states such as Belgium and the Netherlands are divided into regions where modernization has taken different courses. In the United States existing geographical differences from North to South were reenforced by the progress of both industry and the slave plantation system. In fact, the most socially upsetting effects of early technology came from Eli Whitney's cotton gin, which made it possible to profit from slave cultivation of short staple cotton. This changed slaves from relatively low-profit workers who might soon have been given freedom into an urgently needed labor force. Except for the ginning of cotton, the technological explosion in the United States from 1780 to 1850 involved chiefly the Northeastern and nearby Western areas.

Encouraged by state governments that reflected the deep cultural drive for utility, technological improvements in all spheres of activity came rapidly. Some came even too rapidly as impatient entrepreneurs overburdened themselves with too many diverse investments. Yet, viewed in retrospect, the period 1783 to 1800 was one of revolutionary advance. In 1800 there were banks and insurance companies chartered by the states, hard-surfaced turnpikes and canals, and flour milling, the largest export industry, had been completely automated by Oliver Evans. On the Brandywine River of Delaware and Pennsylvania there were some sixty water-powered mills of various types. By 1790 a steamboat had run on schedule on the Delaware River, although it was not well enough financed to overcome, through improved speed and reliability, the popular feeling that the competing stage coach lines on either bank were preferable. In 1802 Evans made the world's initial sale of a high pressure (modern type) steam engine.[1]

All these developments were, of course, stimulated by some hopes of profit, but they were brought about more by the "artistic" drives of innovators living in a society in which such action in itself was highly valued rather than by market considerations. Fitch's steamboat, for example, preceded adequate demand. Recent studies have made it appear that American skilled labor was little more expensive than that of Great Britain.[2] The effort to eliminate labor was as much a result of the demands of an expanding market, and cultural values as of wage rates. As a whole, American values were as near to being suited to the technical changes that were made as seems ever likely to be the case. The Pennsylvanian Albert Gallatin, brought up and educated in Europe, said in 1808, "The energy of this nation is not to be controlled; it is at present exclusively applied to the acquisition of wealth and to improvements of tremendous magnitude."[3]

While British society and values offered fewer barriers to change resulting from technology than did those of the nations of continental Europe, it did not absorb such change as readily as did the social values and general culture of the United States. In Great Britain highly skilled handworkers, for example, often saw machinery as a menace whereas the "jacks-of-all-trades" in the United States usually saw machinery more as a means of conquering the environment. Except to a small minority of landowners, intellectuals, or religious fanatics, American ways of life or values did not seem menaced by the machines that produced cheaper transportation, clothing, and household goods. In contrast, many people of Western Europe, in their more rigid occupational and social strata, either deplored the possible social effects of mechanized production or felt a threat to their economic security.

Social Adjustments and Values

There was no clear stage of "protoindustrialism" in the United States: one in which rural mills impoverished farm families by taking away their income from handwork. Expanding American migration, shops and mills could relatively quickly absorb labor displaced from agriculture. To a large degree new industrial workers represented a net addition to the American labor force. These men and women were drawn either from immigration or unneeded labor on family farms rather than from a painful readjustment where jobs moving from home to factory might mean economic hardship for the home or unpleasant changes in work styles. Hence the United States absorbed early industrialism with less cultural or social readjustment than was necessary in Europe—and with only minor changes in indigenous cultural values. Relative lack of a depressed laboring group allowed the old value of individual responsibility for success to remain strong with little change in other values.

This was largely because American agrarian values were already suited to capitalist business. As Francis J. Grund, an unusually keen observer from Austria, wrote in 1836: "Business is the very soul of an American. . . . Neither is this hurry of business confined to the large cities . . . it communicates to every village and hamlet and extends to and penetrates the western forests . . . it is as if all America were one gigantic workshop."[4] In fact, the economic changes of the period before 1850, including those brought about by early railroads, tended much more to reinforce the traditional American cultural values inherited from the earlier centuries than to menace or supersede them. Machine shops, urban factories and country mills became ever larger with up to five hundred or six hundred workers in a few instances, yet plant supervisors were generally in direct contact with proprietors. Before the railroad corporations became large, there was no substantial group of middle managers. Good supervisors often performed many small jobs in the plant. Consequently, supervisors, even in large factories, were usually motivated by values inherited from the artisan shop. Early American mill proprietors were chiefly criticized for not clearly seeing management as a separate function and for not giving its needs sufficient thought.[5]

The continuing American pattern of rural mills retarded adjustments in values and interests to changes in what one might say were beyond the older scope of perception. The interchange of goods over rivers, roads, and canals between country and city around the big East Coast ports was building each of these centers to several times its size in 1790. But with a few exceptions new urban problems received little attention. The poor in these fast-growing cities, many of them recent immigrants, became more numerous and needed more relief, but they received relatively less. Increases in expenditures for sewers, drainage, and police and fire protection lagged in the biggest centers and were neglected altogether in many smaller ones.

Within the growing cities, social life went on much as it had since their beginnings. Although some writers in each generation have foreseen industrialism's bringing major changes in family life that would alter the basic culture, actually the changes of patterns and values in all but a few families from 1780 to 1850 do not seem to have been of major importance. In most areas even the small percentage of the population working in rural mills preserved the nuclear family pattern with its normal transfer of cultural values as it had been earlier in America. Migration continued to be a major factor in family life. Such movement tended to minimize the effects of factory employment by making it temporary, the average worker staying less than a year on one job and in many instances moving directly back to farming.[6] One can guess that an immeasurable number of children were exposed to both millwork and farm work with the latter not only embracing very many more families, but likely in all but a few instances to be the rule over much longer periods. As seen by European observers, the American family continued to be a democracy with lax parental authority. Such home relations probably tended to enhance individual initiative and responsibility, together with resistance to arbitrary authority of the kind that is necessary in bureaucratic structures.[7]

Little was done about extending public schools before the 1830s. Education of the young remained largely dependent on the intellectual and financial resources of the individual family. Outside of southern New England, free schools were generally for urban paupers. By the 1830s the upper-income groups of the big cities and the members of the small, skilled craft labor unions were beginning to see virtue in free education, but for opposite reasons. The craft unions wanted education in order to aid their children in rising in the world; the upper-income group hoped to indoctrinate children, particularly those of poor immigrants, with respect for law and the social structure. Not until after the writings and speeches of Horace Mann, as commissioner of education for Massachusetts in the mid-1830s and early 1840s, were many businesspeople convinced of the value of paying taxes for free education before workers entered apprenticeship.

Once in school, children usually learned with the aid of Noah Webster's texts—the speller after 1783, the grammar by 1784, and the reader in 1785. These books, particularly the reader, were filled with the social philosophy that only property conferred real worth or satisfaction and that the road to this happy state was through hard work and saving.[8] In the 1830s the McGuffey readers began to compete for the school market. They also stressed self-help, the sanctity of property, and Christian morality. The admonition that "one doer is worth a hundred dreamers" reflects an enduring cultural value.[9] The mastery of the external was, and probably still is, valued more than the enlargement of the aesthetic, the imaginative, or the learned "internal."

Law and Values

The same values and spirit, in different language, shaped American law. Carefully analyzed, law inevitably reveals much of a nation's system of values and norms of conduct, as well as its problems or social pathology. Though initially based on the traditional laws and practices of Great Britain, from whence most immigrants had come, the substance and inherent values of American law had started to diverge as soon as the early settlers brought legal actions. In contrast to the feeling in older nations, law was not seen in the colonies as an eternal set of principles expressed in customs and derived from natural law. Rather it was a means of expediting everyday controversies and speeding development. In the North there came to be a pervasive legal bias in favor of the active operator, the entrepreneur, as against a passive or absentee owner. The judges, selected in the North from the local political leaders, were essentially lawyer-businesspeople. In the South, the value placed by the planter class on aristocracy confused the situation. Many judges were slaveholders who were probably more likely to follow the aristocratic landowner biases of the English common law.[10]

But it would be a mistake to think in either region in terms of the use of actual common law precedents. Even by the mid-nineteenth century a New Hampshire justice boasted: "We regard the ignorance of the first colonists . . . as one of the most fortunate things in the history of the law . . . we happily lost a great mass of antiquated and useless rubbish and gained in its stead a practice of admirable simplicity."[11] In the nation, as a whole, there were few learned justices. Consequently, legal decisions reflected more than usually the current values of the society rather than ones from some distant past. The emerging state judicial doctrines were more a current and popular "common" law than were the disregarded English precedents. During his nine years as chancellor of New York (1814-23), the famous legal analyst James Kent said that he never heard an opinion of one of his predecessors cited.[12]

As may be surmised, state sovereignty over statute law, interpreted with every judge his own oracle, could lead to quite different codes and decisions. Fortunately, the common cultural values, the possibility of the appeal of interstate cases to the federal courts, and the fact that most business was located around a few ports made decisions tolerably uniform within at least each major trade area. For example, New England courts tended to follow the decisions of Massachusetts, and those of New Jersey, New York, and Pennsylvania tended to follow each other.

American economic and other values may be inferred from marked differences from English law. One of the most abiding of these was antimonopoly. Starting as early as cases against river steamboat operators' associations in 1818, various state courts ruled that *any* mutual attempt to fix rates was a conspiracy in restraint of trade whereas British courts condemned such actions only where they seemed contrary to the public welfare. This manifestation of the stronger emphasis on individualism was still to be an issue in the 1980s. Intense local feeling, another lasting cultural value expressed in law throughout the nineteenth century, discouraged achievement of uniform precedents by appeal to the federal courts. Not until 1842, in *Swift* v. *Tyson*, did the United States Supreme Court declare that in cases accepted on appeal a uniform national common law would be applied.[13]

Another type of conflict between the values of expanding business and localism came over the right of eminent domain, particularly for canals and railroads. A solution adopted in the areas of most active building was evaluation of the individual's property loss by local committees. This practice lasted until nearly midcentury. In the early days of the new governments, business disputes were also handled by special local tribunals. Such practices, as well as equity and the traditional use of juries, illustrate the strength of popular, communal values exerting pressure on the law as compared to either the traditions of Great Britain or the tighter legalism of countries using derivations of Roman law.

Bankruptcy and the collection of debts based on commercial paper were major causes of discrepancy in laws and decisions from state to state, but by 1840 the accepted forms and doctrines were becoming tolerably uniform. It is interesting that the largest industrial and mercantile states, New York and Pennsylvania, had the most lenient bankruptcy laws, again illustrating the American value placed on the active operator. Peter J. Coleman writes: "It would probably be a bit too much to say that every American was a latent robber baron . . . but the pendulum of opinion swung from hostility to bankruptcy relief to an attitude that mixed indifference with tolerance and outright approval."[14] The fruits of such cultural values would be evident in legal actions later in the century.

Values in Politics

A full understanding of the negative value later placed on government, particularly that of the nation—a set of beliefs so severely challenged by events of the 1980s—needs to be based on a long view of American history. The conventional ideas of a rise of local democracy during the Revolution, a return to government administration by the upper class under the new Constitution, and professionalization of politics from 1820 to 1850 still appear reasonable. As population spread westward, the last phase of the cycle was reenacted again and again. At the start the town and county would be run by the initial developers and successful merchants. As the community grew bigger, time-consuming public administration would be consigned to professional lawyer-politicians, indicating that business success was more valued than political prestige.

The colonial cultural trait of distrust of distant governmental authority continued to operate against granting authority to Washington or faraway state capitals. This meant, in turn, that less value than in Europe was attached to holding national or state office. Before Richard Nixon, no president of the United States has ever been attacked more disrespectfully by the opposition press than was George Washington. The ability of the states to agree on an effective form of central government was in doubt for more than a decade after declaring independence from Great Britain.

There is a basic conflict between the strong American

value placed on individualism and equalitarianism on the one hand and the practice of effective government, which in its operation must be administratively firm rather than democratic. As in other nations, the people elected to state or national office either were already, or soon became, upper middle class in their associations. Government by average "people" is impossible in practice because upward mobility through the political ranks necessarily gives the successful politician above-average interests and goals. Thus, there was probably as wide a gap in America as elsewhere between political ideals or values and actual political performance.

Granting the problems and contradictions of democracy in a world where aristocracy or class structure was still tacitly accepted, the new federal authorities may have gained from relative popular disinterest. But American political performance was hindered by problems more severe than the inevitable social distance between the majority of the ruled and their rulers. In an age of little education and slow travel, the average citizen thought in terms of his or her neighborhood or at the most a part of his or her state. Transcending and complicating this localism were well-established regional loyalties based on differences in some inherited values and current interests. Slavery set the states from Maryland on south apart from free states to the North, and cotton and sugar, in contrast to wheat and tobacco, made a less deep rift between the upper and lower tiers of Southern states. New Englanders were proud of their literacy and their scholarly religious heritage, which set them apart from the more polyglot and presumably less "cultured" people of the Middle States. In the early West, settlers from each region inevitably tried to take their cultural values with them. Some change would have had to take place in the West from their new surroundings, but in addition many "older" Americans clashed with recent German and Irish immigrants.

Whereas regionalism and localism produced conservatism or resistance to remote authorities, migration tended to engender indifference even to local politics. To the man or family who didn't plan to stay any longer in an area than was needed to show a good profit on the purchase and sale of land, even local politics were of slight interest. Similarly, it was often easier to abandon buildings and go elsewhere than to repair and improve them.

Both the increase in the prosperous but landless urban population and the relative equality of settlers in new areas led to a gradual breakdown of property requirements for participation in the voting process. Furthermore, the universal free male franchise was a logical extension of the value placed on "popular democracy" and extolled by orators on July 4 and other patriotic holidays. Even a slogan repeated for generations is bound to instill a cultural value for some part of the population. In other words, though successful Americans might value liberty and equality of economic opportunity more than democracy, they recognized the legitimacy of the latter. The new voting rights may be symbolized by the male suffrage provision in the New York State constitution of 1821 and the lack of property requirements in those of the new Western states after 1819.

In federal politics regionalism, localism, and the economic opportunities of private life operated to restrain national powers and diminish the prestige of national offices and indirectly of all people in government. Indicative of regional jealousies was the inability of the federal government to pursue any consistent tariff policy. The same state jealousies prevented large-scale federal expenditures for internal improvements. When William H. Crawford, as head of the federal Treasury Department in 1820, found there was no effective resistance to using federal offices as a reward for political help, he started what was later called "the spoils system." It is easy to see political practice, both state and federal, during the next decade as a result of the low value Americans put on remote political service, in sharp contrast to the high prestige and security of tenure that rewarded central government officials in Europe. This was also in part a reflection of the cultural values that impelled Americans away from public service and into profit-making enterprise.

Another strong factor in reducing federal prestige and leadership after 1815 was lack of fear of an attack by any powerful outside aggressor. Oversimply, Americans saw little need for a strong, efficient national government, and after the railroads produced a national business system, many citizens saw less need for state government. This situation might have put great value on good municipal and county administrations. Here continuous immigration and domestic migration undermined wide and active public participation. Even by 1900 the average length of residence on a Middle Western farm was about five years. So, as in the case of federal or state, only second-rate people or those with some personal interest to advance devoted time to local politics.

An Example of Local Values Against National Interest

One of the clearest effects on national development of the excessive valuation of regional and local interests was in banking. Scared by the financial breakdown at the end of the War of 1812, Congress chartered a Second Bank of the United States. After seven years of initial difficulties, largely regional or local in origin, the Bank came to be at the head of the best banking system the nation was to have before the late twentieth century. Nicholas Biddle as president of the bank from 1823 on saw his role as that of a central banker. Through over twenty branches the bank supplied nationwide and foreign exchange and tried to police the currency issues of local banks by demanding redemption when the amount of notes issued seemed excessive. Biddle did not, however, have the powers necessary to make the bank a last resort in case of financial trouble. He could not create cash in return for government bonds or use measures to take responsibility for saving local banks from failure. Yet the controls Biddle used in the interest of national and international stability alienated the state bankers who wanted to use risky loans for local development.

In successfully vetoing the rechartering of the Second Bank in 1832, President Jackson symbolized the victory of local interests over the needs of a stable federal financial system or of regional and local sympathies (values) over national order. The following year the high tariff majority in the House and Senate similarly capitulated before the threat of South Carolina to secede from the Union. Ultimately, in 1861 regional loyalty in the South was to prove a cause men would die for rather than continue their ties to the Union.

Returning to the example of banking, after the end of the federal bank, conflicting state laws threw national finance into twenty-five years of confusion that were ultimately completed by the coming of the Civil War. As in banking and the law, state autonomy and local sentiment posed difficulties for all interstate business, but until around 1850 most internal trade was intraregional or across the lines of only one or two states, so that banking was probably more disrupted by localism than other business.

Westward Migration and Localism

Most families moving westward did not go to a vast unoccupied frontier; rather, they settled when possible near other newcomers. Almost everything dictated such settlement. The federal government opened new land for initial sale only in limited areas. The land investors who bought at the government auctions wanted to create compact communities; even the "squatters," those hardy migrants who settled in advance of the government auctions, wanted to be as near as possible to each other so that when the government put the land up for sale, they could count on community support against "outside" bidders for their acreage, allowing the squatters to buy at the minimum price. Wise developers of the new land

generally strove to develop community centers through helping to locate stores and churches. Because this was very profitable business, if successful, a Main Street lot bought for $1.25
per acre from the government might later sell for several
dollars a front foot; it was pursued by local agents repre-
senting Eastern investors.

The result of such cooperative endeavor between capitalist
investors, land agents, farmers, and sundry business or religious interests was a strong and competitive local spirit. Each
township area could gain greatly from roads, canals, churches,
schools, stores, newspapers, county offices, and, after 1840,
most of all from a railroad station. If the town prospered
and acquired a hotel, a newspaper, and possibly a college,
each of these institutions was viewed as a way of advertising
the community and increasing its business and land values.[15]
Continuous migration nourished local enthusiasm and diminished criticism of local abuses. Newcomers to the town
or city had come there because they thought it offered more
opportunity than their previous home. Because they were
largely dependent on making friends and "fitting in" as soon
as possible, they were not likely to be critical. If after a few
years a migrant found his or her environment uncongenial,
he or she left rather than try to reform it. Perhaps nowhere
in the world has there ever been such great value placed on
glorifying the locality.

The loyalty to local institutions survived far beyond the
early stages of development. Business clubs were formed that
tried to turn small cities into big ones through free loans
and cheap land to enterprises that would locate in the town.
Internal critics of a city continued to be regarded as dangerous pariahs who were working against the welfare of their
neighbors.

Perhaps no governmental bodies have ever been as akin to
risk-taking small business as those of the newer inland cities
of the United States. Practically all expenditures had to be
justified as likely to help local economic interests. A college
or a church would attract more people to the town and bene-

fit local merchants. A railroad station or a county seat was worth bidding for with local money, but sanitation or various types of protection that cost money with no immediate prospect of cash return were neglected. Therefore a "risk-taking" society assumed such hazards to safety and health rather than increase taxes. These values instilled in the citizens of new settlements greatly reenforced the negative value placed on social welfare and the positive ones on individual risk and success.

In centering attention on westward migration, it must not be forgotten that migration from Europe to the United States was continually reintroducing people of various Old World cultures to the American mixture of values and norms. In the decade 1845 through 1854, the numbers of immigrants, chiefly German and Irish, exceeded domestic births. Because a large part of the Middle States port city populations had always had immigrant origins, these new infusions seem to have made relatively little change in the main values of American culture, partly because these values had come from, and were strongly supported by, the midcentury American environment and partly because the indigenous values had absorbed the pressures of diverse national traits almost from the beginning.

Although American culture was perhaps no more regionally differentiated or localistic in values than that of, let us say, France, the place of localism in the total complex of values was basically different. French localism and regionalism came from centuries of family living in the same place, of interrelated families, and inherited customs peculiar to the locality. In the Eastern United States both North and South, the stay-at-home families of the older areas exhibited some of the French provincial values. But to the West, and all America beyond the seacoast had started as "West," the localism was aggressively future-oriented rather than tied to the past. Strong national governments also controlled localism in France, where national judicial, civil, and military services were present and dominant in every area whereas in the United States the few federal marshals or courts were beyond the view or interest of ordinary citizens.

In adjusting to the more integrated national life of the twentieth century, therefore, American localism presented different problems and reactions from those of the national states of Europe. In a very broad generalization, one may say that the American culture of the late eighteenth and mid-nineteenth centuries, with its extreme values on local progress and personal fulfillment through making money, reached a maximum of difference from the values of Europe.

Regionalism and Religion

In general, analysis of cultural values is easiest and most reliable when dealing with the effects of relatively stable institutional or physical elements in the environment, particularly those that control physically measurable change or stability. By such criteria, religion poses difficult problems. The strength of belief depends much on family training and, therefore, has a strong element of perpetuation where devotion is already strong. But in the period from 1740 to 1830 many families of each generation were making alterations in the details of their beliefs, and there is no real measure of the types of changes or the basic reasons for them.

One factor is certain: Sparsely settled frontier areas could not support elaborate churches. Therefore, the westward movement generated individual evangelists and circuit riders who moved from town to town and area to area, evoking fears of hell and damnation by highly dramatic performances. Such self-appointed ministers were also popular among the "poor white" and black populations of the South. They preached a self-, not a socially, directed faith.

During the half century following the Revolution, Baptism, Methodism, Unitarianism, Universalism, and Deism also spread, but, in the early part of the period, orthodox religious enthusiasm was thought to be declining. Emerson's famous statement that in New England from 1790 to 1820 there was "not a book, not a speech, or conversation or a thought" worth noting illustrates the quiescent attitude of the Eastern ministry. Afraid, however, of losing the newer parts of the country to the evangelical Baptists and Methodists, the Presbyterian and Congregational denominations made joint efforts after 1800 to send properly trained ministers west. Thus, the period after 1800 appears to have been one of spreading religious revival, but as Alexis de Tocqueville wrote about 1830, "some profess the doctrines of Christianity from sincere belief in them, and others do the same because they fear to be suspected of unbelief."[16]

The deism or agnosticism popular among the upper classes of Europe in the late eighteenth century, often referred to as the Enlightenment, had few followers in the United States except among leading intellectuals such as Franklin or Jefferson.[17] In any region a reputation for Christian belief, regardless of sect, was good for social, political and business standing. There was also a "civic" or "public" belief in God, invoked by statesmen on solemn occasions, which was above denominationalism.[18]

There appears to have been no conflict between the various Christian doctrines and the cultural values placed on self-help and success from equality of opportunity. As a consequence, in studying the effect of cultural values and norms on American historical change, we find that those stemming from Christian doctrine may usually be assumed to be relatively stable and representative of a widely held background of moral values.

An Age of Optimism

In comparison to those of Europe, the inherited values and norms of the United States seemed well adjusted to the pre-1850 stage of the new society. European culture subordinated the possibilities opened up by machines to contradictory values that were either not strong in America or not even present. Sociologists say that where social structure is relatively permissive, technology and other physical factors will guide change. But the ease of acceptance of machines and factories seems to have gone beyond the flexibility of the social structure. The impulses and values necessary to create the new order were unusually strong in American culture. By the beginning of the new century even the leaders of liberal agrarian thought such as Thomas Jefferson were vigorously advocating manufacturing.[19]

The problems of crowded industrial areas, of business bureaucracy, and of technology too intricate for the mechanic to understand were only faintly recognized by 1850, and machines were expected to end poverty and its problems. With just a few exceptions, enterprises of all types were managed by proprietors or partners who knew their workers and rewarded efficiency. The cultural values of self-improvement, the quest for opportunity, the virtue of work were functioning with unusual strength.

General American agreement on the value of sociotechnological advance is indirectly attested by the comments of foreign travelers and the complaints of New England literary men between 1830 and 1850 on American manners and society. These observers give the picture of a confident, businesslike, morally bigoted, self-satisfied, and relatively uniform society in, at least, the North and West. A French aristocrat said in the 1830s: "Without devotion to business, without this constant direction of the energies of the mind to useful enterprises, without those political and religious notions that repress all passions but those whose objects are business, production and gain, can any one suppose that Americans would ever have achieved their great industrial conquests."[20] These God-fearing citizens who accepted few social responsibilities appeared to Europeans as models of material success and spiritual confidence. A British visitor of the period said, "In that knowledge . . . which the individual acquires for himself by actual observation in ordinary avocations of life, I do not imagine the Americans are excelled by any people in the world."[21]

PART II

THE CHALLENGES
TO OLDER VALUES
1850-PRESENT

4

Growth of a Nation

Despite regional variations and the growing influence of the frontier and the older West, the traditional American values had by 1850 a recognizable degree of national uniformity. Not only de Tocqueville and Grund but also the acerbic Mrs. Trollope, who stayed longer in the South than in the North, spoke of Americans as one people. Whether in the North or South, the culture was the product of more than two centuries of people with northwestern European origins living in a series of settlements that were mainly tied to the activities of the Atlantic coast. Although specific values and norms differed, particularly from South to North, there were surprisingly large uniformities in activities and attitudes toward life. Of the famous eighteenth-century Virginia planter William Byrd of Westover, Michael Zuckerman writes that "his enterprises were so often commercial and so infrequently agrarian."[1] White citizens in all regions believed in the unique greatness of America, in some version of democracy, in racism, utilitarianism, activity rather than contemplation, material success under capitalism, and Evangelical Protestant religion. European travelers would find Philadelphia or Charleston primarily "American," and only secondarily would they detect a number of regional differences. In all, though there were local variations, there was an old and well-established culture that reflected a set of core values.

Using Jules Henry's distinction between drives and values, one can say that the values placed on action per se, individual success, and freedom supported drives that would be hard to alter whereas a value such as that placed on a limitation of the scope of government action could change from one period or situation to another.[2] For example, a New York State Canal Commission of 1811, headed by wealthy aristocrat Gouverneur Morris, reported that "for purposes of more efficient administration, the commissioners . . . indicated their preference for public rather than private management." "Large expenditures," they concluded, "can be made more economically under public authority than by the care and vigilance of any company."[3] This statement, which was probably agreed to by the upper class that largely staffed politics at this time, shows not only the early distrust of private corporations, but also the absence of education in the later doctrine of laissez-faire. American values were not being contradicted; they had simply not been formed by or, applied to, such areas.

The Inevitable Challenge of Urbanism

Cities necessarily had to be partially contradictory to complete freedom of enterprise, individual responsibility, or a general policy of laissez-faire. But for more than two centuries the conflicts between community regulations and individual freedom of action were too small to bother the chief maintainers of social values. In 1790, with population still almost entirely in the coastal states, all urban population (people in places of over 2,500) was about 5 percent, and dwellers in the congested areas of the three large cities, Boston, New York and Philadelphia, were only about 2 percent of the total. By 1850 urban population reached 15 percent of the total; and by 1900, 40 percent. As urbanites approached half the population, their most serious problems began to force local or state government to take new regulatory actions.

In reality, cities had from the beginning been in need of regulations that would have challenged the then current American values. William Penn's concept of a city kept green by widely spaced streets and well-separated houses broke down at once from lack of "zoning" regulations on the use of property. The faster cities grew, the more they needed regulations, but even slow rates of growth produced what Lewis Mumford has called "unbuilding." To understand the inevitability of this process, one will find it helpful to see types of land use in the growing city as a series of concentric circles. Trade and manufacturing are normally at the center, surrounded by worker housing and then by middle-to upper-income residences; it is clear that no inner circle can grow except by invading the one that surrounds it.

There are many types of modification of this overly neat plan, introduced by rivers, hills, and other natural features that produce unusual configurations; but the conversion of old buildings to new uses goes on where factories or shops spread to new areas, narrow streets become inadequate, industrial waste accumulates, and run-down buildings become parts of the growing city. Critics have claimed this process to be most extreme in the United States because of rapid growth and continual migration.

The decline of once tolerable housing into slums had been going on in the big port cities from their early days. In 1850, Charles Dickens wrote of a New York slum: "See how the rotten beams are tumbling down, and how the patched and broken windows seem to scowl dimly, like eyes that have been hurt in drunken frays. . . . Where dogs would howl to lie, women and men and boys slink off to sleep, forcing the dislodged rats to move away in quest of better lodging."[4]

To such inevitable physical destruction of unregulated cities was added the social challenge of thousands of immigrants with cultures and values varying from those of the natives and in the twentieth century of large numbers of blacks brought up in the South and conditioned to a special type of agrarian society. Hence among large parts of the urban population there was little or no support for the old values based on laissez-faire and individual self-regulation. The growth of cities had to be planned to prevent self-destruction.

In contrast, most of the big cities of Europe had been planned to some degree from their beginning as fortified trading posts that needed protection from feudal warriors and frequently had been replanned by the sovereigns of the later national states. Consequently, urban problems were a special American example of a challenge to traditional values, and by the early twentieth century the United States was a nation of cities with their metropolitan areas, while the farm population had become a shrinking minority.

Rural-urban antagonism with its effects on cultural values and norms had already become the subject of numerous scholarly analyses and much outstanding poetry and fiction. Obviously, such a deep-seated challenge to established types of personality and values was manifested in many ways. For example, on the physical side, no state government had considered financing the construction of farm or rural housing because traditionally neither "equality of opportunity" nor "welfare" warranted this. Yet in the cities, the private, market-oriented supply of houses proved dangerous to public health and welfare. By 1900 conditions in the worst urban slums challenged belief. Nowhere else in the world were there slums as concentrated as those of New York City. The first efforts in Illinois and New York were to cure menaces to public health from excess sewage and inadequate amounts of air by municipal regulations. This approach worked poorly. The courts generally held that existing property could not be condemned for failure to meet new requirements yet new construction that would meet the regulations was too expensive to compete with the old overcrowded, run-down buildings.

By the 1920s, local and state tax relief was being offered

to promote new housing, but again the new buildings attracted middle-income tenants, and the poor took over additional superannuated structures. Hence, in contrast to the leading nations of Europe, the United States up to 1937 had failed to meet the challenge or urban "welfare" or adequacy in housing. Only the depression of the 1930s forced federal action to remedy the world-famous "American slum problems." The Wagner-Steagle Act of 1937 appropriated money for federal construction of housing for families of limited income, and by 1940 the urban slum problem began, for a time, to be alleviated. In 1949 a federal statute offered cities two-thirds of the cost of slum demolition to clear space for educational and other desirable urban developments. Neither of these laws worked well for the slum dwellers. Government-built, large, high-rise apartment buildings constructed in place of former slum neighborhoods destroyed community relations and encouraged crime. After some twenty years the policy was abandoned in favor of renovating old houses, but the restoration of neighborhoods once held together by stores, saloons, schools, and churches was seldom achieved. In fact, the first stage of development often put slum dwellers out of their homes with no proper planning for location elsewhere. All the programs challenged older American values such as self-determination, individual responsibility, and limitation on action by government.

Normally, cities grew from inmigration rather than from local fertility. In the nineteenth century more people went from country to city than went to the frontier. The immigrants to the cities from Europe and the blacks from the South came largely from rural areas. Consequently, a process of acculturation from rural to urban values was continuously going on, and the needed adjustments such as more reliance on government, more education, and more collective social agencies, if accepted at all, lacked deep roots.

Some values threatened by the impersonality of urban life led people to seek substitutes. Important among these was the desire to "belong" to a meaningful group, familial or otherwise. Such attachments could be taken for granted in agrarian small-town culture, but, in the city, different bases for groups had to be found and almost inevitably group attachments were weakened in the process.[5] Instead of a community of longtime village associates as a meaningful (or reference) group, the urban dweller had to substitute less intimate acquaintances met at special occasions, and the family, becoming less of a twenty-four-hour environment, lost supportive strength. This has been held by social scientists to generate a feeling of "anomie," or alienation because of lack of any satisfying sanctioning group. Clubs, lodges, and fraternal organizations, as well as churches, helped to meet such needs. Often the immigrant church was as much a social as a religious center.

By the early twentieth century, American sociologists were fearing that the family would be a casualty of urban development. That this has not happened is an example of the fact that there is a rough hierarchy in the force of various values and that those established at an early age and those close to self-preservation and gratification of the ego are far stronger than those taught at school or work. The nuclear family has thus far long outlived those who predicted its dissolution.

In a very broad view, it may be said that, up to modern times, Western World culture was predominantly a rural culture and that the values, customs, and habits appropriate to cities have everywhere challenged older traditions and values. Yet because of the lack of much experience with the values of centralized control and planning, inevitably accepted by most Europeans because of wars and absolute monarchies, the needs of urbanism have been harder to meet in the United States. These needs have challenged the deeply held American values of freedom and extreme individualism.

Economic Challenges to Superior Progress

Together with urbanism, the vast territory acquired by the Mexican War and the Oregon Settlement, along with the simultaneous coming of railroads, were to offer challenges to older patterns of American economic development and inevitably to the associated values. Instead of a nation extending across fertile lands from the Atlantic Ocean to the Mississippi Valley, the United States suddenly spanned the continent. The "Great American Desert," so-called in earlier years, now had to be integrated into the life of the nation. The old, relatively compact America of midcentury probably led the world both in its standard of living and in the rate of increase in real income per capita. Britain, its only close rival, was slipping back. That Americans would thrive more than any other people was a profound, almost universally held belief. The fact that over the next century and a quarter the size and infertility of much of the continent, combined with rapid growth in population, slowed the increase of real income per capita more than in other leading nations was only recognized by scholars about 1960.[6] It took the energy crisis of the 1970s to bring the challenge to the old beliefs home to the general public.

Relative prosperity up to 1930 had blinded Americans to the superior rate of economic growth per capita in nations such as Germany, Japan, Sweden, and—at times—even France. Growth in the production of goods was so rapid in all leading nations that self-satisfaction was widely shared, and Americans readily confused the massive total growth of their economy, which was by 1900 larger than that of any other nation, with superiority in relation to growth in per capita income. Preserving and advancing "the American standard of living" had become a major cultural value often used as a justification for temporary evils, such as denials of civil rights to striking workers or wasteful exploitation of resources. Placing this high value on production was central to what has been called America's doctrine of "business laissez-faire," to which growth and prosperity were customarily attributed. The belief in being a nation of unique plenty was still strong in the Americans of the 1980s.[7]

Only in the early 1960s, when American economic statisticians such as Simon Kuznets and Robert E. Gallman began to extend tables of national growth rates for the leading industrial nations backward to the 1840s, was there awareness of the comparatively average per capita performance of the United States. Granted that long-term growth rates are difficult to measure and that stages of economic development have to be taken into account in drawing conclusions, it became clear that the United States from 1850 to 1960 was not the leader in increasing per capita income. Neither did the distribution of American income before 1930 seem more even among various levels, a factor that might compensate the average person for slower growth. Gallman, the principal authority on United States national product in the nineteenth century, concludes as follows from data supplied by Kuznets and others: "The growth of American national product per capita . . . was not exceptionally rapid. Between 1834-43 and 1944-53 . . . the average decade rate was just under 16 percent. Of the eleven countries . . . [studied], four exhibited rates of growth substantially higher (19-28 percent) and three substantially lower."[8] Gallman knows the limitations of such estimates, but he found that the rank orders remained the same under many alternate types of calculation.

Impediments to Economic Growth: Increasing Population

It seems reasonable to assume that in spite of abundant high-grade raw materials, much fertile land, cheap immigrant labor, and the continuing favorable drives and values of the old culture, the United States was not, even in the best periods after 1855, a precocious world leader in growth rates of production per capita. This conclusion, buttressed by statistics, explained by numerous factors, is quite contrary to the national legend that existed and continues to exist among all but the few students specializing in economic growth. The historical evidence suggests that in the 1970s the United States did not suddenly lose some previous economic or technological supremacy but rather that resources became more expensive and management failed to meet changing costs and foreign competition. Examination of the chief causes of retardation in earlier times will help explain the apparent dilemmas of the 1980s and may serve as a background for a historical examination of which values were most severely challenged.

One distorting element, leading to exaggerated ideas of prosperity, was the casual reporting on American conditions by foreign visitors. Both this group and Americans writing about Europe were almost never qualified to make economic or technological comparisons. Rapid population growth and migration that in either case required the buying of new equipment for home life, farming, and industry gave an impression that everything in America was newer and, therefore, of more advanced design than in the old countries. There was also a strong and probably true emphasis on Americans as "no nonsense" utilitarians and on foreigners as shackled by tradition.

The following suggestions of retarding elements should not obscure the almost steady upswing in American per capita income in the century after 1855. One reason the United States was not a leader was the fact that, except for Great Britain, the economies of other leading nations were in earlier stages of industrial development. Such leads and lags are inevitable in rapidly changing technology, but it is useful to analyze some major reasons for America's difficulties.

The aspect of newness noted by Europeans was true, but the technology was not better. The process of coming to and building on previously unsettled land was a voracious consumer of capital and necessitated higher saving and productivity to equal the per capita growth of long-settled areas. A striking comparison would be that of a large Belgian steel mill that was housed in old church buildings whereas all American newcomers, such as the Illinois Steel Company, had to build from the ground up with consequently larger capital costs.

Although the Civil War put a burden on American development temporarily greater than any similar event in the other leading nations, it was a setback that had been somewhat compensated for by 1880.[9] A more striking fact is that comparative American growth in per capita income did not improve substantially in the presumably great period of advance from the 1880s to 1914, probably trailing Germany by a substantial margin and France by a smaller one.[10] Until 1931, a high rate of increase in population continually retarded the growth of per capita income. In spite of large influxes of adult European immigrants ready to work, domestic fertility kept the number of minor dependents high. And even though immigrants were mainly of working age, they still needed new housing and a wasteful period of adjustment to American conditions.

Other Impediments: Localism and Regionalism

Development of the vast continent called for unprecedented capital commitment and the federal system and localism continued to prevent the easy movement of money between areas and hence the best adjustment of capital investment to savings. Jeffrey G. Williamson has concluded that in the late nineteenth century, in a nation presumably short of capital, useful investment lagged behind savings.[11] Surplus saving occurred chiefly in the Northeast whereas new capital investment was needed in the South and the West. The lack of a central banking system or reliable national security markets available to the small investor hindered the transfer of savings to where they were most needed to promote growth.

The so-called "national banking system" failed dismally as a means of capital allocation. Never designed as a banking system, but rather, in the National Currency Act of 1862 and its amendment in 1864, as a means of forcing unwilling banks to buy government bonds, the law restricted the issue of bank notes to those establishments that subscribed to a minimum of $50,000 in federal securities, and it taxed all state bank note issues out of existence. The "system," therefore, amounted merely to meeting certain arbitrary standards for investment of a bank's own capital and for federal control in these banks of the reserves required against loans. Even interbank lending was condemned by the federal controller of the practices of national banks in 1890. With such onerous restrictions on national banks (so named in a law of 1871), it is not surprising that small state chartered banks, mostly with under the nationally required $50,000 in capital, soon arose and gradually solved the problems of doing business on the basis of checks. By 1887 there were more state than national banks, and by 1910 the state organizations were two and a half times as numerous in a financial "system" with some 25,000 separate banking institutions.

Because only national banks could issue bank notes and, except in the old sea-ports, banking by check grew slowly, in the rapidly developing inland areas there was a chronic shortage of currency. Interest rates, even in major Western financial centers such as Chicago or St. Louis, were 1 percent or more above those in New York or Philadelphia; and in fast-growing rural areas, still higher, if funds were available at all. With farm mortgage lending far exceeding that of any other nation, there was still no secondary mortgage market, that is, no routine, established way for the owner of a mortgage to raise money by selling the certificate.

This lack of any real banking system would probably have had to be corrected in the nineteenth century had it not been for the rise of the New York banks, both chartered and private, which acted as facilitators of the movement of funds. The city banks accepted deposits from the "country banks" and, in turn, made it possible for these banks to finance imports and for their "country" depositors to borrow money in New York. Put another way, the New York and, to a lesser extent, the Baltimore, Boston, and Philadelphia banks of all types helped to make possible a poorly organized but essential nationwide exchange of commercial credits.

This effort was hampered by state banking laws that may be seen as parts of the historic efforts to protect overly valued local interests against the intrusion of more efficient "outside" financial institutions—and often within the states to protect the business of the small-town bankers against the banks of the state's major cities. In Illinois, for example, no Chicago bank could have branches. As late as the 1970s only California and North Carolina freely allowed branch banking. This restricted movement of funds both nationally and within states illustrates that both J. W. Kendrick, who finds a late nineteenth century trend toward increased saving, and Kuznets, who suggests the possibility of shortage of capital per worker, may both be right.[12]

The Federal Reserve Act of 1913 sought to provide better liquidity for banks throughout the nation and access to cash when needed. Its failure to achieve a unified and safe banking system before the 1980s will be discussed later. The point of the whole discussion is the fact that even after 1913 the value associated with localism and state's rights continued to hinder American financial and economic growth.

The same state and local interests operating in politics may also have been a deterrent to development. Corrupt state and city governments enabled some local businesspeople to buy special favors in the way of franchises and permits. These led to development, but usually not in the most economical way. They also led to an adversary relation between most businesspeople and politicians, and, in addition, corruption added to the expense of dealing with government.

Localism could also menace interstate business and investment by making contracts difficult for out-of-state parties to enforce in local courts, and states occasionally retarded international investment by laws against ownership of land by foreigners. That these government practices, particularly corruption, were recognized and disapproved of by honest businesspeople is indicated by the fact that many of the "Progressive" reform movements of the 1890s were initiated by business clubs and organizations.

In spite of some precautions written into the U.S. Constitution, such as the interstate commerce or sanctity of contracts clauses, the states continually managed to interfere with the free operation of a national market by local taxes and regulations. California, for example, has clean air laws differing so much from the national average that motor vehicles must be specially equipped. Pennsylvania counties collect a personal property tax on the dividends paid to its citizens by companies that have not paid a state registration fee. There are scores of other state regulations affecting interstate commerce.

But far more serious is the mere fact of three layers of government—local, state, and federal—where other advanced nations have, effectively, only two. It means more government officials and agencies than voters will watch, more honest claims on the taxpayer's dollar, and still more opportunities for corruption. These governmental duplications mean that the taxpayer gets less for his or her money than in many other industrial nations. All in all, a strong value placed on local interests, understandable in the light of history, became a menace or hindrance in a highly industrialized society.

More Impediments: Size and Distance

Overshadowing all other handicaps to rapid growth in individual income was the vast size of the country with its high mountains, broad deserts, and widely dispersed farmlands and natural resources.[13] Although, as Frederick Jackson Turner proposed, the moving frontier may have promoted democracy and other desirable values of the traditional American type, its continuous settlement and resettlement were economic drains. Economically, instead of being a "unique" American advantage, the "continual rebirth" used up great amounts of capital for new homes, farms, mills, stores and communications.

This cost of the process of settlement was a problem faced from the earliest colonization by the companies of London on into the twentieth century. Without the introduction of new farm machinery, such as complete harvesters, which greatly increased the productivity of labor, the process of bringing distant Western land into use might have been prohibitively costly. In any case, a more restricted westward movement with more utilization of land in large farms near industrial centers would probably have led to faster economic growth than the one promoted by the federal Homestead and Distribution acts, the railroads, and the land companies.

Quite aside from the details of how development might have been better managed, there was the unalterable fact of great arid and mountainous waste spaces and immense distances. All the rapidly industrializing parts of Europe, excluding Sweden, could be put in the northern United States between Boston and Detroit. The excessive distances uneconomically inflated the statistical rate of American growth in per capita income. A railroad a thousand miles long has higher total freight costs for the same amount of traffic than one 100 miles long and, therefore, produces more gross earnings for moving the same amount of goods. But if the shorter road does the same job of bringing things to market, its smaller returns represent a greater gain, not a loss. For example, in 1900 the United States with only a slightly larger national product than imperial Germany had ten times the ton miles of freight.

W. Paul Strassman points out that concentration on the needs of transportation, the American investment in railroads from 1850 to 1890 about equaling that in all manufacturing, took many of the potential innovators and investors away from other sectors just as a high investment in military equipment would have done.[14] For example, mining copper in Utah and refining it in New Jersey add a considerable transportation cost to the product as compared to mining in Cornwall in England and processing at nearby Swansea in Wales.

As a consequence of this inevitably continuing situation, the OPEC oil embargo and price increases of the 1970s had a more serious effect on the American economy, which was geared to long-distance highway and rail transportation powered by oil, than on very compact industrial rivals such as Germany and Japan. The results were these: adding to the already great strains of shifting employment from manufacturing to service; adding greatly to a serious inflation; and, in all, producing challenges that American industrial management failed adequately to meet.

Kuznets contends that the rate of increase in per capita product in the industrial nations "was due primarily to improvements in *quality* of inputs . . . greater efficiency . . . traceable to increases in useful knowledge and better institutional arrangements for its utilization."[15] These factors, which may be simplified as technology, education, and business management, will be discussed in subsequent chapters; but they are all adversely affected by distance. Distance, for example, presents internal problems in transferring new technologies from one region to another; advanced education is difficult for students in sparsely settled areas; and management of distant operations is likely to be less efficient than those in the central office.

A Background for Challenges

The process of occupying such a vast expanse of territory was not only an economic disadvantage, but it also slowed or prevented the development of values suitable for dealing with the problems of the late twentieth century. Although one cannot generalize about the culture and values of the "frontier" as a whole, because much depended on the values and habits the settlers brought with them, the continued migration appears to have encouraged some common characteristics. The settlers on each new frontier were generally from an older area only a hundred or two hundred miles East, that is, from a previous frontier. Therefore, except when Europeans such as Scandinavians or Germans moved West from the immigrant ports or New Englanders went West for business reasons or to "free" Kansas, the frontier was a continuous process of revising values generation after generation to fit the needs of a relatively primitive society. At the worst, it developed traits such as "large scale waste, a nearly pathological restlessness or discontent with the environment which resulted in perpetual migration . . . and furthermore a suspicion of intellectual activity, contempt for the arts, insistence on conformity, cultivation of the social function of the churches as a substitute for religion, a leveling of education . . . ," and a universal and continual consumption of liquor by all, including women and the clergy.[16] On the good side, the frontier encouraged generosity, respect for women, the nuclear family, and easily made friendships.

From the mid-nineteenth century on, a large number of the bearers of the older American culture had to readjust their values and resulting activities to these new "frontier" norms. That Americans did so tolerably well is a testimony to the flexibility of the older values and to the perpetuation of the high values always placed on utility and personal success.

But the history also shows that the "crisis" of the 1970s and 1980s is not something sudden and revolutionary. Rather, it represents an accelerated increase of problems that in less obvious forms have challenged Americans for more than a century. The dramatically swift upsurge in Japanese technology since the 1960s has been partially similar to the challenge of Germany in the late nineteenth century. The dilemmas of how to educate have never diminished. The problems of big management have increased with the size of the companies, but have been present ever since the coming of the railroads. Effective government by many "sovereign" states of a vast, greatly differentiated area has also grown more difficult with the new social and economic demands of a mature industrial society, and it involves problems that historically neither the United States nor other nations have satisfactorily solved. Studying the evolution of these problems and the resulting continuing challenges to cultural values should help to clarify the elements in the present situation, one that is generally blamed too much on short-term social or economic maladjustments.

5

Bureaucracy

Challenges to older, American values came merely from having to carry on many types of activities in government and society on a larger scale, one necessitating values suitable for working in and managing big, impersonal organizations. American morals and values were those of the farm or small trade center, where people met face-to-face; where success seemed to depend on visible energy and effort; where most businesspeople knew each other; and where loyalties or duties other than to community, church, and family were taken lightly. In contrast, during the years after 1850 the new scale of development put more value on prestigious positions, loyalty to an organization, scientific knowledge, and long-range planning, none of which were widely valued in America of the mid-nineteenth century.[1]

Ending all fear of an attack by a Western Hemisphere nation, the victory over Mexico and the end of the Civil War allowed Americans to concentrate on internal self-development. There were no external pressures for loyalty to the state, no high prestige for the military, no demand for sacrifices in the name of national preservation. In this absence of external pressures, the American standard of living began its century or more of rivaling Christian doctrine as the ultimate sanction for any course of action.

Weakness in Government Bureaucracies

With the Mexican War greatly adding to the vast areas of unused land acquired earlier by the Louisiana Purchase, the 25 million Americans of 1850 were challenged to make economical use of an area six times the size of non-Russian Europe. Perhaps without the railroad, this continental domain would have broken apart. President Polk, at least, feared so in 1848. Even by building frantically until 1855, railroads made connections only between the major cities of the East Coast and the nearby Middle West. To govern and develop such a mammoth nation would have challenged the best of European bureaucracies with their hereditary administrative elites and their firmly controlled clerks. In the United States it overwhelmed the small, poorly organized administrative organizations of the territories, state capitals, and Washington.[2]

In contrast to earlier days, American culture was now partly responsible for slow or poor adjustment to change. The historic emphasis on individual rights as opposed to obligations, on quick ad hoc decisions rather than on careful analysis, and on the importance placed on monetary success as against artistic or scientific acclaim—all rested on values that were not well suited to the large scale impersonal bureaucracies, public or private, necessary to govern and supply this continental empire. For such reasons, as well as because of a disregard for complicated "book learning," little advantage was taken of the European literature on public administration.

Cultural values that for centuries had stressed loyalty to higher authority, both military and civil, put the European bureaucracies in a different position in relation to both internal personal ambitions and the individual's relations to society. In Europe and the rest of the world, government service of any kind was the most prestigious career that one could choose, and allegiance to the official hierarchy was not only accepted but exalted as one of the highest values. Most Europeans strove only for a social "place" in life rather than for an open-ended career promising personal wealth, and to them a government post was a highly satisfactory status.

In America, government posts were largely state and local, weak in power, low in salary, and lacking in prestige. So probably there was little useful knowledge that even conscientious readers could have absorbed from European writings going back to Machiavelli on the management of public bureaucracies. The acute French observer de Tocqueville implied that basis of American's weakness as bureaucrats in his statement: "not only does democracy make every man forget his ancestors, but it hides his descendants and separates his contemporaries from him; it throws him back forever upon himself alone and threatens in the end to confine him to the solitude of his own heart."[3]

Aside from the Civil War and its aftermath, the most pressing large-scale administrative problem in America from mid-century on was the transfer to private ownership of nearly two billion acres of public domain through the federal land office. Because of American cultural values on individual success and personal initiative, only political hacks who had not succeeded were likely to be satisfied with a job in this branch of the federal bureaucracy. Although they may have failed in the outside race, these people still shared the cultural drive for personal wealth. Consequently, two types of trouble confronted the grantee, purchaser, or homesteader of government land: (1) honest loss of titles through land office inefficiency, and (2) supersession of proper titles through land office corruption. As a result, many families seeking new land found it safer to buy from a railroad or land company that had received a validated federal grant than to settle on government land that would supposedly be allotted freely after five years' residence under the Homestead Act of 1862. In all, by 1890 only about 20 percent of the acreage transferred from the government to the private ownership of actual farmers had been freely acquired.[4]

The land office in Washington was merely a spectacular example of the failure of government bureaus all over the country to attract people capable of dealing judiciously with the rise of new railroads and other corporations that were politically powerful compared to their historic predecessors. In some states, the rise of big companies led to the control of the legislature by bosses, chiefly responsible to certain corporate businesses; in other states to battles for control of legislation in the interest of small local businesspeople, including farmers; and in still other cases, to manipulation of legislators by railroad or lumber companies and other big interstate corporations. Because, as in the case of federal bureaus, able people did not seek careers in state government, the result of these pressures was to reduce efficiency in state administrations to its lowest ebb by 1880. The state courts, aided by the able business lawyers who practiced before them, seem in retrospect to have been the forces that prevented a real breakdown in public authority.[5]

Both lack of need for strong defense and corruption at all levels led to the rise of an "adversary" attitude by taxpayers toward their governments. It may be argued that this was one of the values inherited from nearly two hundred years of colonialism; yet in the early nineteenth century the hostility to government was notably absent, particularly on the state and local level. Government was looked to at that time as an aid to economic development. The adversary attitude seems to have arisen when governments no longer did much for economic growth and were suspected of serving corrupt special interests. The perpetuation of this attitude or negative value into the late twentieth century stands in contrast to the readier and often more effective use of government in other advanced industrial nations. Andrew Hacker thinks that "Americans have always tended to view government as inherently illegitimate . . . government has always been weak in America. The problem is not oppression, but a climate that prevents government from doing a decent job."[6]

Bureaucracy Challenges Older Values

In the United States before 1840, only a score or so of big mines or mills had a "middle" or bureaucratic type of management, one large enough to have levels where important decisions were neither made nor executed. With the coming of the railroad companies, many more Americans had to adjust their cultural values and behavior to the norms or roles expected of well-paid employees who exercised little initiative in their jobs of merely passing on orders from above. The railroads, using new and experimental technology and moving many middle managers far from the head office, were an especially hard school in which to learn the internal values that reconciled one to a life of custodianship, one of executing orders and of protecting or enhancing the value of other people's property.

As in government, the problem has remained, a far deeper one than designing effective forms of management. Two centuries of American cultural emphasis on working for one's personal advantage; approving an individualism stressing civil rights, not allegiances or duties; and a steady emphasis on social equality were all inimical to efficient service in large business organizations, which have always operated as dictatorships. Because the historic processes had made Americans "masterless and separate," there was, and has continued to be, a tension between the deference system necessary to the smooth running of an authoritarian bureaucratic organization and normal Americans.[7]

In addition to such impediments, other American values hindered adjustment. Important among these was the same aversion to book learning on the part of "practical people" as in the case of government. As the *Baltimore Partriot* observed at midcentury, to business leaders, "a book or treatise upon the management of railroads would be an intolerable bore."[8] Furthermore, learning from European experience required not only translation from French or Geman into

English, but usually it required applying precepts developed in public administration to somewhat similar problems in business. There was some European writing on governmental administration of business, such as French accounts of the practices of the tobacco monopoly in the seventeenth and eighteenth centuries, which would have been very useful, but which was, of course, not even known of.[9]

Basically ambitious Americans did not want to recognize or adjust to the problems of big organizations. A half century later, Andrew Carnegie felt and expressed the same anti-bureaucratic feelings. He said to students at Cornell University: "Is any would-be businessman before me content in forecasting his future, to figure himself as laboring all his life for a fixed salary? Not one, I am sure. In this you have the dividing line between business and non-business; the one is a master, and depends upon profits, the other is a servant and depends on salary."[10] Nevertheless, more and more aspiring Americans had to work their way through the new bureaucratic forest of paperwork, orders from above, and both subtle and positive limitations on choices and conduct. Because the business corporation has never been democratic, there is a degree of irony in the fact that the initial rise of corporate hierarchies came during the period often referred to as Jacksonian Democracy.

In 1841, the federal government had 18,000 civilian employees, who were divided among several departments. Within a decade, large, expanding railroad companies employed as many as 5,000 each, more than in any single department of civil government. The only important transfer of administrative knowledge between government and business was in the form of some efforts by the latter to learn from the practices of the army, but it was soon discovered that the absolute autocracy of this service, enforceable by punishment, had little in common with efficiency of command on railroads, where free Americans could not be subjected to the military type of penalties. Fortunately for the historical study of the

early challenge to American values brought by railroad bureaucracy, the chief contemporary commentator, Henry Varnum Poor, was both a fine representative of the older culture
and also one of America's ablest business analysts. A graduate
of Bowdoin College; a Maine lawyer; a friend of Emerson,
the Channings, Parker, Ripley, and other Massachusetts
leaders of the "New England Renaissance," he thoughtfully
represented historic American values.[11] In his middle thirties,
he first became involved with railroads by helping his brother
John Alfred Poor in the building of the Atlantic and St.
Lawrence Railroad from Portland, Maine, to Montreal.
Upon completion of the road in 1849, Henry's brother
bought the *American Railroad Journal*, published in New
York City, and Henry accepted the editorship, a post he held
until 1862. Within five years, Poor had directed the *Journal*
toward the study of management, and his writings brilliantly
illustrate the protest of the bearers of the older values against
the new challenges. As his biographer Alfred D. Chandler,
Jr., puts it: "For Henry Poor . . . the efficient construction
and operation of the American railroad system was even
more a moral than an economic necessity."[12]

Although both government and business bureaucracy involved the problems of loyalty to influential superiors and a
reasonable work ethic in an impersonal hierarchy, the management of big corporations also came inevitably to involve
ultimate power in the hands of people who were not the
principal owners of the enterprise. "By the end of the 1850s
Poor was tracing nearly all the problems of the railroads to
the underlying fact that their managers did not own and
their owners did not manage."[13] On a very simple level, this
ambiguity meant that a person with a relatively small investment might control the policies of a large railroad, as did
Erastus Corning, president of the New York Central, and
have it buy its supplies from his wholly owned mercantile
companies.[14]

But beyond such practices involving conflict of interest,

which came within a few decades to be recognized and condemned, the professional manager had different personal
goals and values from those of the owning proprietor. The
manager who built a career in a large corporation put a high
value on security and on a good reputation for careful trustee-
ship rather than on risk and innovation. Because the gains
from risk-taking innovation would accrue chiefly to the mass
of stockholders, while failure would be blamed on management, taking risks was often avoided. This problem was less
obvious concerning the railroads, forced by competition into
vigorous growth, than it was to become in another century
for management of oligopolistic corporations in comfortable
adjustments to relatively stable markets.

Like Carnegie, Poor always found it difficult to believe
that any person on a salary would do more work than was
necessary to collect regular wages. Incentive was even less
when a person was in the pay of a large organization, for
here "all of a similar grade receive nearly the same rate of
compensation although some of the parties instead of being
valuable officers may possess no qualifications for their
duty."[15] He thought that until some way could be found to
reward individual merit, "railroads, wherever they may be,
will drag along in their beaten tracks of dullness and routine, and become worse managed and less productive year
after year."[16]

A trip to England in 1858, where Poor found similar railroad problems, impressed on him "the grave difficulties of
adapting human capabilities and current business practices
and institutions (the existing cultural values or norms) to the
severe requirements demanded by the efficient operation of
large-scale administrative units."[17] It is worth noting that he
includes not only railroads but all large-scale bureaucracies.
Surely nineteenth-century Americans were amateurs at such
adjustments compared to the long-trained professionals of
Europe.

Professional Management: A New Order

In the long run, a reasonable degree of honesty and of accountability was imposed on railroad corporations by an excess of government regulation, which only increased the lack of incentive in bureaucratic managements. These problems were never solved either for the railroad or other giant companies. The old saying that "a man won't work as hard for the railroad as he will for himself" remained true, first of the roads and then of other big "publicly owned" companies. The American value on individual initiative and responsibility still existed in the late twentieth century and was still ill-suited to bureaucracy. As Michael Kammen observed in 1971, "The American is more preoccupied with private or personal values than with social or political ones. . . . By contrast, in most other countries there is a greater concern with corporate loyalties and more personal involvement in corporate issues."[18]

Lack of proper incentives for middle and upper management and criteria for promotion have been in varying degrees worldwide problems, but lack of security in such a career was peculiarly American. In the European and Japanese cultures, fixed statuses, each of which had its rights and privileges were both accepted and valued. Government and business provided lifetime careers from which people of the managerial class were severed only by unusual events. Companies did not normally expect to bid executives away from each other. As late as the mid-twentieth century, there was no equivalent in Europe or Japan of the American market for trading in managers.

In the free and individualistic United States, there was from the beginning a steady flow of managers from company to company. One might see it as reflecting the cultural values on self-determination and growth, as well as resulting from the practice of continual migration. Railroad superintendents who made a good reputation were bought away by a higher salary on another road, and those who made poor decisions or enemies among superiors were fired without severence pay. Looked at one way, American business employees never had the job security, either in high or low positions, that may have been a long-run cultural heritage of the fixed statuses of feudalism in European and Japanese cultures. That, in spite of probably adverse economic effects, movement between jobs is probably an enduring part of the American cultural heritage, stemming largely from migration and new opportunities, is underlined by its persistence to the present day. Lester C. Thurow noted that in 1980 the average United States manufacturing firm lost 4 percent of its work force every month. This made companies reluctant to invest much in "on the job training" because it seemed cheaper to bid skilled workers, technologists, or managers away from other companies by higher wages. "If anyone, workers and managers," writes Thurow, "is basically on his own when it comes to economic success, how could anyone expect the American corporation to have a long time horizon?"[19] Yet long-term calculations were increasingly necessary for keeping up with advancing technology and changing world conditions.

In spite of such lacks in suitable managerial values, the large spread-out national market and the importance of the size of shipments in winning low, long-haul rates from transportation companies had made America a leader in developing multiplant corporate bureaucracies.[20] The Standard Oil Company, which was greatly aided by special railroad rates, has been the subject of intense, scholarly, historical study. The Hidys, official historians of the company's early years, found that the top corporation, controlling scores of subsidiaries, was only loosely coordinated and depended a great deal on making policy through informal conferences.[21] The organization, having developed over time, continued to reflect the mélange of companies based on historical precedent, personal predilections, state corporation requirements, and tax laws.[22]

Although Standard Oil, with its near monopoly position

in the domestic market of 1900, continued profitable, many of the jerry-built big business corporations formed by mergers in the late 1890s and early 1900s were not. The general failure of the American corporate executive to adjust to more study and careful advance planning rather than rely on hasty action and to rely too much on increasing size to overcome market difficulties finally led to modern management study.

Business Faces Its Bureaucratic Challenges

The reluctance of active, powerful business leaders to study from books or reports what they felt they already knew by instinct was a continuation of time-honored American attitudes and values. An early movement toward conscious study started at the worker-supervisor level, where, according to the old values, the workers involved, by the very fact of still being laborers, had obviously not been properly motivated to succeed. The original aim of "systematic" study was to get more work out of labor without interfering with higher management. Frederic W. Taylor of Philadelphia was the best known of the early twentieth century writers on what he renamed "scientific management." Taylor and others undoubtedly improved on existing shop procedures, but this had little effect on bureaucratic problems. By the 1920s it was fairly clear that there was more leeway for improvement in higher management than there was in the shop, and this implicitly challenged the doctrine that getting ahead in big companies was in itself a proof of superior ability or diligence. New theories, such as the widely accepted one of Elton Mayo, saw productivity more as the result of managerial relations to the production processes than of a work-ethic in the laborers.[23] This is one of the little noticed major changes in the values of industrial society (capitalist or socialist), a change perhaps greater in its impact on values in the United States than elsewhere. As a General Electric top executive said to me forty-odd years later, "We spent the years up to

1930 trying to get more work out of workers and from then on trying to get more work out of management." Reflecting the cultural value on practicality, the initial development of acceptable new theories of business control came from active participants rather than from the writings of scholars.[24] It may also have been true that the national culture, which had values least in harmony with those emphasized by bureaucracy, needed the most authoritative arguments for adjusting to new practices.

The first influential American analyses of big management came from the chief executives at E. I. du Pont de Nemours and Co. in the early years of the century, and then more strikingly at General Motors in 1921. In the recession of 1920, overly optimistic management by the impetuous William C. Durant had left the big automobile company with excessive inventories and a shortage of working capital. Because the Du Pont company owned a controlling block of 27.5 percent of General Motors common stock, Pierre S. du Pont; his assistant John J. Raskob; and their bankers, the House of Morgan, were able to dictate a solution to the situation.[25] Pierre S. du Pont was already familiar with practical thinking about the problems of top management, and he recognized in the plan of Alfred P. Sloan, a General Motor's executive, a structure for lessening the company's problems.

The immediate solutions for General Motor's financial troubles were a Morgan loan and the economic recovery of 1922, but the "Sloan Plan" gave the giant corporation an altered system of management based on a more rational approach to the problems of organization. Authority was delegated to divisional managers, who would be limited chiefly through budgetary control by a group of top officers. In other words, the plan involved in theory divisional autonomy in both the manufacturing and marketing of different products, but central control over large expenditures or purchases. In addition, a central staff was set up that could give advice to divisional managers on anything from engineering to accounting, but the managers did not have to heed such advice unless ordered to do so by the president of General Motors.

This plan devised by practical executives came a generation later to be a major theoretical base for academic study of management in America, which on the practical level of studying actual business operation preceded such courses in Europe. One solution to this paradox that a culture placing a low value on intellectuality was able to produce leadership in new theorizing is that the United States with its spread-out big companies had worse problems than the Europeans. Another solution is the fact that most of this writing was the application of empirically oriented American social science, as distinct from more philosophical European thought, to practical business problems. It belonged more in the realm of social technology than in that of any philosophy of human relations on the level, for example, of Max Weber in Germany.

Another view of Sloan's solution, later called the "M" or multidivisional form in contrast to the "U" or unified form of management, is the fact that its promise was never wholly fulfilled. In General Motors and other companies, the top echelon of managers, who were not connected with any division, continued, in fact, to guide many lower-level policies of the company that involved changes in practice or expenditure. From 1950 on, individuals with training in accounting became more and more numerous among this top level of managers, and short-term tax and profit considerations, "the bottom line," tended to take precedence over improving the efficiency of the product or other long-run considerations.[26]

Fundamentally, as long as dictatorial power emanates from the top—and no management expert has ever suggested a democratically run business or government bureaucracy—the basic problems seen by Poor regarding the railroads remain.[27] Corporate promotion in any culture may depend more on having a friend at a higher level than on ability, which often can't be measured for the individual. Good social relations, friendliness, a good golf game can be more important than elusive characteristics of intelligence or ingenuity, traits that may actually antagonize associates and superiors. Technical improvement of managerial hierarchies can serve to reduce friction and improve communication, but many weaknesses seem imbedded in human nature rather than resulting from particular American values.[28]

In large corporations that achieve oligopolistic market control, particular challenges from bureaucracy appear. Research and development investment may be used to suppress innovations that will upset the stability of either the organization or its market, as in the case of the fluorescent light blub in the early twentieth century and of the small or electric automobile in the third quarter of the twentieth century. But these are only conspicuous examples of a process that goes on subtly in smaller instances. In companies with good control of their market, the value placed on organizational harmony by top management has also led to higher wages for organized labor than the economy as a whole could sustain. By striking at one of the companies that jointly controlled pricing, a union often got increases that would necessarily become effective in other companies, with the additional cost passed on to the consumer. By the late twentieth century, the problem of how top management of very large companies might pursue the culturally approved goal of personal wealth was sometimes solved by large corporate mergers. Because by this time insiders were forbidden by law from using their superior knowledge of coming events to speculate in the stock of their own companies, they tended to take advantage of the generally accepted practice that the bigger the company, the higher the salaries and bonuses that top management could be paid by friendly boards of directors, sometimes staffed in the majority by managers themselves. Hence merger with another large company operating, in some cases in a different field, would justify general top-level salary increases and perquisites merely on the basis of increased size.

This could explain some mergers that seemed to promise little, if any, increase in either market control or productivity.

Ubiquitous Challenges

Because each type of production, marketing, and service led to somewhat different forms of management, it is hard to define the total challenge to older values and customs. Similarly, there seemed little correlation between management forms and profits. Study in the 1950s of a sample of one hundred British manufacturing plants of various sizes and types developed no close correlation between adhering to the most advanced theories of management and commercial success.[29] It appeared that successful performance of managerial roles depended, as Max Weber had suggested, on charismatic leadership at least as much as on structure and definition of duties. Although there were, of course, elementary principles such as respect for channels of authority and clearly defined delegation of power that were generally adhered to, on the level of overall successful coordination, management appeared more an art than a science. As a consequence of this variability, comprehensive understanding of the new values and challenges stemming from the managerial as distinct from the proprietary role developed slowly.

Study of this evolving role and its challenge to the values stressed in earlier chapters may begin with noting how individuals properly qualified as managerial artists were conditioned while struggling to reach the top, and this, in turn, involves the apparently enduring problems of bureaucracy. The qualities needed to get ahead in the organization were loyalty; unquestioning acceptance of hard work; good judgment; outward adherence to the social norms; a friendly, genial, but decisive personality; and, in a really big corporation, some luck in becoming visible in a favorable light to men higher up. Some of these qualifications such as hard work or good judgment accorded with earlier values, but the majority did not. David Sarnoff as president of the Radio Corporation of America in the 1950s said: "The most important factor in determining whether a man is really a satisfactory employee . . . is . . . his family life; if he has a normal happy family life, a good home, he is a satisfactory normal fellow."[30] At about the same time, C. H. Buford, a railroad president, advised an aspiring young man to "cultivate and develop a pleasing personality . . . show interest in other people and what they have to say."[31] William Stephen of Goodyear said the same thing in a different way: "We can't consider a man for promotion unless he has built a smooth running organization."[32] Frank Abram, the chairman of Standard Oil of New Jersey, recognizing the reciprocal influences in a bureaucracy said: "Modern management might well measure its success or failure as a profession in large part by the satisfaction it is able to produce for its employees."[33]

The Bureaucratic Society

Granting the challenge of bureaucracy to older American values, let us consider how much of the population has become directly involved. There are no exact figures on the number of individuals performing managerial roles in either large government or private organizations. Of total employment, government service takes up about 15 percent, chiefly in state and local governments, and the less than 2,000 corporations in all lines of business big enough usually to be listed in *Fortune* employ under 30 percent. The big business companies are heavily concentrated in manufacturing, which is a relatively declining area. Consequently, from the standpoint of employment, the majority of employed men and women work for companies too small to be regarded as wholly impersonal bureaucracies, and as the economy continues to move from manufacturing to service, the relative number should increase. Among policymaking top executives, the same situation is true to a greater extent. The thousands of men who run the very big companies are few compared to millions of proprietors, partners, or executives of small enterprises.

Consequently, only a minority of economically successful Americans are really faced with the bureaucratic challenge to traditional values. Yet, in fact, the challenge is broader than that. Big companies control the nationwide media of communication and make their values and customs appear to be the prevailing ones. Few well-educated Americans realize that most people work in small establishments or that the large companies in semidurable consumer goods are chiefly assemblers and marketers of parts made by hundreds or thousands of small suppliers. General Motors, for example, has supply relations with over 40,000 companies.

Furthermore, large organizations, both government and private, undoubtedly have a higher level of education among their managerial employees than would be found in smaller business. This aids what writers on contemporary society have called the penetration of the administrative personality into social life, or the spread of "organization" men and women. Society, as a whole, thus becomes more bureaucratic in mentality than can be accounted for on the basis of employment. Among the attributes emphasized are conformity and an aim to please those in control, in obvious contrast to the historic American core values of individuality and equality.[34] An adviser on careers for women, for example, writes: "The associations and friendships reflect managerial values. These imply a degree of distancing from subordinates."[35]

While historic American values have been challenged in adjusting to business bureaucracy, so, in varying degrees, have those of every other industrial nation. Because it has the largest centralized bureaucracy, one would expect the challenge to be most severe in the Soviet Union, where one towering hierarchy is trying to centralize and direct all aspects of life. A relative lack of success suggests the conclusion that many smaller independent bureaucracies function better than a single centralized one. And this raises the questions of what functions have to be conducted by large organizations and what can be more efficiently carried out by small, independent units.

Franchising, as illustrated in automobile marketing, motels, and restaurants, has been one capitalist effort to combine the individual incentive of the profit-making manager with the efficiency possible from centralized purchasing of supplies and the protection of capital advanced through uniform accounting. As already noted, large companies in some types of production buy most of their goods from smaller suppliers. Thus, the challenge of bureaucracy may affect the brand-name companies that assemble and sell the ultimate product more than it does the growers or fabricators of the basic materials.

In government, protection of job careers through civil service regulations and examinations for promotion may make some underlings more willing to assert themselves than in private corporations, but they are also less hopeful of rapid advancement and, therefore, more willing to do work in uninspired, routine ways rather than run the risks of exercising initiative. Perhaps some government bureaucrats work harder than corporate ones, but often less effectively because of rigid or poorly designed regulations and lack of monetary incentives on a par with those in business. Yet, in both spheres, the troublesome problem remains that the groups that define the roles played restrict the enterprise and activities of both colleagues and subordinates. The challenge, therefore, is what incentives can lead bureaucrats to innovative or entrepreneurial behavior?

In all, how to make bureaucracy responsible, imaginative, and effective seems one of the greatest challenges to traditional values and to civilization itself. Bureaucracy's rigidities and inertias menace both government and economic organizations. A silver lining of this presently ominous cloud may be that with sufficient mastery of energy and of production on a technological level, inefficient bureaucratic functioning may become the saving element in providing "work" or employment for growing populations.

By the 1980s the United States, starting with more hostile values, had adjusted to the problems of bureaucracy on a practical level about as well as other nations, but perhaps with less esprit or feeling of achievement. The extreme emphasis of Ronald Reagan on freedom of enterprise is an example of failure to adjust on a deeper level to the bureaucracy in which he functions.

6

The Challenge of Science

The challenge of scientific research, theory, and attitudes to American values took two important forms: (1) a challenge to take the time necessary to think in abstract theoretical terms and imaginary models rather than in terms of concrete practical mechanisms that could be manipulated and improved by mere physical alterations and (2) the challenge of theories of evolution, mutation, relativity, and sociobiology that contradicted or severely challenged the literal interpretation of the Bible, the historic basis for American Christian religious values. In the hereditary culture that held sway until the last half of the nineteenth century, God, nature, and life seemed understandable to the common individual, and God through the Bible had provided a guide for proper conduct. According to these older beliefs, valuing the relentless skepticism of science or devoting the time and energy to the analysis needed to promote pure science seemed either immoral or nonproductive.

The Rise of Science, 1850–1900

In Europe, the nineteenth century had been a period of the unification of science, a time when scientific attitudes gradually became powerful social and educational forces.[1] Except for the use of electricity in telegraphy, the early and mid-nineteenth century English, French, and German scientific knowledge had little direct effect on American education or practice. The historic culture continued to favor the improvement of technology by practical individuals rather than by theorists; and, as we have seen in Chapter 3, technology supplied in its own operations a fertile school for improvement.

Harvard and Yale made some special provisions for the teaching of science in the late 1840s, and a few other colleges provided majors in science or engineering. Only the Military Academy at West Point and Rensselaer Polytechnic Institute in Troy, New York, specialized in engineering in the first half of the century. From 1860 on, the number of engineering schools grew, but there was little connection between their practical instruction and advanced scientific research. The small amount of university research that went on in pure mathematics or science was the work of a handful of individual Americans, of whom the one destined to be the most famous was Willard Gibbs, formulator of the laws of thermodynamics. Teaching at Yale from 1863 to 1902 and, after publication of "On the Equilibrium of Heterogeneous Substances," a man of worldwide reputation, he is said to have had in his whole career only half a dozen graduate students.

As in other nations, arguments for encouraging science came chiefly from people of the middle to upper classes. Manual workers, urban or rural, were seldom concerned with such issues.[2] Among those who could allocate money to research, there was, in general, a professed admiration for the findings of science, but donors showed little inclination to advance money for the lengthy experiments and theorizing that were usually needed for basic scientific progress.

In empirical investigation of matters of some economic importance, the situation was different. An Academy of Natural Sciences was founded in Philadelphia in 1812 to promote the study of natural history. A main interest of the academy was in taxonomy, the identification and description of plants, animals, and minerals; but it also helped to finance exploring expeditions to Greenland, Florida, and the West.[3] Similarly, a practical man like Thomas A. Edison, working by trial and error, was widely acclaimed, but the basic scientific work in electricity had been done in Europe.

In science involving agriculture, the division between pure and applied science was very clear. Starting in 1887, the federal government allotted money for state agricultural research stations. But the scientists working in them applied only well-known ideas from a narrow range of disciplines. To have approached the state administration for the supplies and time necessary for developing something such as the Mendelian laws would have been too hopeless to attempt. "Even the most devoted lay supporters of scientific research in agriculture," writes Charles Rosenberg, "had an ingrained suspicion of abstract research and what they often conceived to be its egocentric and, in a sense, anti-social practitioners."[4] One may say that there was a moral prejudice, or adverse value, against withdrawing from active production to pursue abstract speculation.

As long as pure theory could be imported from Europe, the economic development of the United States was regarded domestically as a more valuable and important use of scarce resources. Before 1900, American business companies sponsored little research of any kind, and college teaching schedules were generally too heavy to allow time for the pursuit of new theory. Yet the prestige of the findings of science were continually advancing. American moralists, for example, were advocating abstinence from both sex and liquor on the basis of the findings of "medical science" with the same fervor that they exhibited in enjoining their interpretation of God's will.[5] After 1900 and particularly after World War I, private foundations, universities, and some government agencies began to contribute to American advances in pure science. Perhaps this did not illustrate any greater cultural value placed on abstract speculation, but rather that World War I had demonstrated in many fields the inadequacy of American theoretical knowledge.

The Mysterious Universe

Regardless of backwardness in most branches of pure science, by the late nineteenth century world developments in widely known scientific thought had strong impacts on American ethical and religious values. While Galileo had upset the theology of the seventeenth century by demolishing the three-tiered concept of Hell below, earth in the middle, and Heaven above, the new seventeenth-century science did not specifically contradict the Testaments, and in New England particularly religion reached a cultural intensity probably greater than anywhere in Europe. As late as the mid-nineteenth century, Horace Mann wrote: ". . . between true science and true religion there can never be any conflict. As all truth is from God, it necessarily follows that true science and true religion can never be at variance."[6] The conflict between religion and science in the late nineteenth century, spearheaded by Darwinian evolution, was specific and unavoidable. Genesis and the new science were literally contradictory. In addition, European biblical scholarship, in applying historical analysis, was demonstrating problems of evidence and reporting in the Testaments.[7] Until the 1890s American seminaries and churches of all types resisted such challenges surprisingly well. The "old-fashioned" religion still held sway in all but a few urban Protestant churches, and Catholics and Jews held to their established doctrines. Consequently, the weakening of religious certainties and religious behavior that had come gradually over generations to Europeans occurred rapidly in America from the 1890s on. And weakening religious beliefs had more effect on the rest of the value structure of American middle-class society than seems to have been the case elsewhere.[8]

The basic challenge to values in America, as in Europe, however, was not Darwinism alone, but also the increasing force of the experimental attitude of science. A series of discoveries around the turn of the century bred in fields as diverse as physics and psychology were more potentially upsetting to inherited values than any scientific findings since those of Galileo. Furthermore, the arguments of the earlier periods had been conducted on the basis that human beings were rational and able to perceive reality whereas now both physical and social science contradicted such assumptions.

Shortly after 1900, physics joined psychology in showing the severe limitations of both verbal logic and sensory perception. The roots of the upsetting knowledge that people could not perceive the nature of the physical world through their senses or describe its processes by verbal logic goes back at least to Clerk Maxwell's work on electromagnetism in England in the 1870s. But the philosophical significance of this earlier work was not clear to many intellectuals before about 1910, when Einstein's field equations based on treating space, time, velocity, and mass as dependent variables began to be widely known, if not understood. More upsetting in the long run to any mental image of the nature of things was the work done by Lord Rutherford, Max Planck, and Niels Bohr in the second decade of the century on the structure of the atom and the nature of energy. The net result was to show that ultimate substance, if such existed, was so infinitely small in relation to the space it seemed to occupy as to be negligible and that what we perceived as matter was an extremely complex structure of energy relationships. As John Langdon-Davies put it, "Science . . . has taken the very ground from under our feet and substituted a nightmare myriad of atomic and solar systems."[9]

All this knowledge was deduced from the interpretation of indirect tests and expanded into theories by mathematical logic. When existing mathematics would not provide answers that accorded with the data, as in the case of Planck's quantum theory, new systems of mathematics were developed. To some devout physical scientists like Episcopalian Sir James Jeans, God could be pictured as the master mathematician.[10]

Although this might seem to go back to the Thomist view of the essential rationality of God, the new rationality was expressed in a flexible mathematical logic incomprehensible to the common individual. It was difficult to convey the new theories even to nonmathematical intellectuals. But the fact that physics had destroyed the old concepts of the universe and its matter was widely known by the end of World War I. The hope that physics had opened the door to a new age of faith was not substantiated. The more general reaction appears to have been a challenge to the human ability to understand the nature of the environment, as well as increased skepticism regarding all doctrine.

Nonrational Individuals

The new social sciences joined in the challenges to perception, verbal rationality, and the universality of "true" moral values. Late nineteenth-century experimental psychological and anthropological study of human behavior cast doubt on the rationality of social systems or values. William James's *The Principles of Psychology,* published in 1890, was one of the earliest books to spread the new scientific ideas. "The human being who appears in James's psychology," writes Edna Heidbreder, "bears little resemblance to the rational man of earlier years."[11] Later in the decade, John Dewey began applying the new experimental psychology to child-rearing and education.

During the next generation, academic psychologists continued to undermine the religious ideas of will-power and rationally controlled activity, but for the educated urban middle class the theories of Sigmund Freud were more dramatic and exciting. The popularity of his ideas in the United States in the 1920s fitted the social trends arising from urban industrialism as well as from the whole complex of experimental attitudes. Historians have pointed out how the initial Freudian emphasis on sexual repression as a primary cause of neurosis fitted well with postwar ideas regarding the elimination of the double standard of morality and more freedom for women. Bringing sex "into the open" went with short skirts and a superficial sort of equality with men in smoking, drinking, language, and voting. But the more important and lasting effect of Freudianism, one that later revisions scarcely weakened, was to reenforce James in challenging the objectivity of reason. Rational processes, according to Freud, were guided by unconscious urges. Given the same situation, two "reasonable" men would, because of different infantile sexual repressions, select facts that led to different conclusions. While ensuing clinical experience and study of the brain have altered these earlier theories, later scholars have not restored confidence in reason and conscious "willpower" as uniform guides to conduct. Ideas have remained ideologies; and truth, relative to its context.

In the United States, particularly, the attack on reason was carried to an extreme. Experiments with the conditioned reflex in animals led the University of Chicago psychologist John B. Watson to advance a system called behaviorism, in which all "thought" was merely the verbalizing of conditioned reactions.[12] The existence of consciousness was held to be a delusion akin to religion, myths, and other superstitions. Though too extreme to convince the majority of experimental psychologists, some big university departments were won over to Watson's views, which were reenforced in the 1960s by those of Harvard psychologist B. F. Skinner. Because Watson was easier to understand than Freud and more concerned with normal psychology, many middle-class parents became behaviorists. Behaviorism also influenced writers on child-rearing and was specifically incorporated in *Infant and Child Care,* a booklet widely distributed in the 1920s by the U.S. Department of Labor.[13]

While Watson made all morality a matter of conditioning rather than thought or will, Freud, in effect, turned old-fashioned American morality upside down. Repression of self-indulgence by the use of willpower in order to abide by divine precepts was now seen as psychologically dangerous in the case of the young and probably futile in the case of adults. The repressed desire would find some alternate and perhaps more subtly dangerous form of expression. As in the case of Freudian ideas about sex, the new morality or amorality of indulgence suited other trends. A relatively mature industrialism in the 1920s was emphasizing greater consumption. Because from 1923 on, lower-income purchasing power per capita was scarcely increasing, greater consumption had to come from luxury spending by the upper-income groups—those who were most influenced by the new psychological ideas.

So the older American moral values of abstinence, frugality, and saving were challenged by a wider acceptance of promiscuity, high consumption, and living on credit. As with behaviorism, later attitudes have modified some of the extremes of the 1920s, but the scientific view of mental processes stimulated by James's and Freud's theories remained the rule in medicine and the social sciences.

The Challenge in Religion and Child-rearing

For the ordinary citizen, the twentieth century changes in attitudes resulted in alterations that were often subtle but basic. The advanced Protestant churches in the larger cities tried to minimize strict doctrine and move in the direction of rendering social service by means of Sunday schools, parish houses, social clubs, and missionary work aimed more at social than religious values. As the ministry became more influenced by the ideas of the parishioners, the successful preacher in a prosperous urban or suburban parish sought to achieve a good adjustment by being a good businessperson and a good social leader rather than a proclaimer of eternal laws. In urban congregations educated Protestants (and one might say the same for Jews) came to apply some of the questioning attitudes of science to their religion. Faith survived, but it was in the background. It was not the active, implicit faith of the mid-nineteenth century. Parishioners valued their church as a social institution, doctrine was approved more pragmatically on the basis of its credibility and utility, and church attendance was seen as a social as well as a religious ritual. The offspring of the immigrants who poured in at the turn of the century tended to have similar views. "The church to them was often one of the many ethnic institutions that should be maintained."[14]

Invading the old-time religious preserves of child-rearing and education, the experimental psychologists, psychoanalysts, and educational specialists sought to perpetuate modified values through altering personality in the ensuing generation. Because material on child-rearing practices is notably absent from biographies and autobiographies, change must be chiefly inferred from the written advice offered to parents. Analysis of some of the available literature from 1865 to 1929 shows the same tempo of scientific invasion of this sensitive area that is illustrated in other conceptual systems.

In the nineteenth century, parents were primarily urged to teach children to know right from wrong, to be respectful of authority, and to be reverent toward God. In order to be fit for the life hereafter, children were particularly trained to avoid the many guises of evil. The naughty child should be told: "You have grieved your parents but you have grieved your Heavenly Father much more, you must ask Him to forgive you and to help you to be a better child."[15] There was still the assumed unity of divine and natural law establishing what was right and wrong. "Unity in nature and man is the moral, pedagogical and religious solution of our time," wrote the veteran educator Emma Marwedel in 1887.[16] The religious tone in the period before 1890 was no doubt strengthened by the fact that a large part of the advisers on child-rearing were women and ministers whereas very few were doctors.[17]

By the 1890s the new psychological ideas were lessening the emphasis on strict, arbitrary discipline and increasing advocacy of freedom of expression for the child. In the Preface to Felix Adler's *The Moral Instruction of Children,* in 1895, W. T. Harris, commissioner of education wrote: "The new ideal regards insight into the reasonableness of moral commands as the chief end." By about 1905 the effects of the new scientific attitudes were beginning to be apparent. There was more emphasis on introspection by parents, and original sin and depravity were generally rejected. On the whole, however, Geoffrey H. Steere has found that the admonitions were still in terms of divine will and recognized principles.[18] Attitudes toward sex differed little from the "Victorianism" of the nineteenth century.

A generation later, the revolution in advanced child-rearing had occurred. The predominately religiously oriented child-rearing text was an anomaly.[19] The measures advanced were generally in terms of psychology or physiology. Writing in 1920, the editor of *Mothers Magazine and Home Life,* came out squarely for experimentation. The child "cannot learn it by looking at it simply or listening to words that adults use to describe it."[20] He warned the mother that "the more she limits her child, the more she handicaps him in his struggle to learn the world in which he must live." He urged parents to be friends with their children rather than disciplinarians.[21] In contrast to the clergy and lay persons of the earlier periods, the authors were mainly doctors. Though there was an emphasis on permissiveness for the child and self-study for the parent, no principles were stated with the unquestioning confidence of earlier times. Authoritarian parents of the old religious type could find little support in the textbooks where Freud's attitudes toward sex training were usually present. Either explicitly or implicitly, children were being trained not for the hereafter, but for practical adjustment to a changing present.[22]

The great world leader in undermining the old moralistic, authoritarian schooling was John Dewey. Because he was also an instigator of rebellion in philosophy and the social sciences, Dewey is probably the most ubiquitous American representative of the attack on older values. His whole system of thought in both philosophy and education was based on the methods of experimental science.[23] He called the elementary school that he organized at the University of Chicago in 1896 "The Experimental School." The next year he wrote: "It is impossible to tell just what civilization will be twenty years from now. Hence it is impossible to prepare a child for any precise set of conditions."[24] Suspicious of all attempts to erect a hierarchy of values, Dewey could obviously not supply the basis for a new structure of belief.[25]

His great influence on public schools occurred through the work of disciples after World War I. In 1904, Dewey had come to Columbia, where Teacher's College was the major graduate training center. A National Society for Progressive Education, formed in 1919, and educational articles and textbooks by his Columbia colleagues, such as William H. Kilpatrick and Harold Rugg, spread the doctrine of child-centered education. Though few public schools could afford a completely progressive system, the Dewey principles were known, perhaps in exaggerated form, to every well-educated teacher. Child-centrism reached its peak in the 1920s and then declined, but the strong emphasis on community relations that survived it was scarcely nearer to the old inculcation of fixed moral values.

Science also influenced education through quite different channels. The scientific management vogue popularized by Frederick Taylor from about 1910 to the 1920s was reflected in educational administration. In 1911 the National Education Association appointed a Committee on Economy of Time in Education, which issued four widely read reports

between 1916 and 1919. Their major emphasis was on elimination of nonessential studies.[26] School boards subjected
teachers' activities to job analysis, and the uses of school
funds were studied on a "scientific" accounting basis. In the
resulting rise of school management, the teaching function
tended to take second place. From the management standpoint, the function of the school was to prepare useful, conventional citizens. To a degree, this was the opposite of the
aims of progressive education, but both shared in the attack
on older educational values.[27] Both attacked the traditional
content of education; both replaced indoctrination in Christian morality with an emphasis on community relations. The
study of languages declined; political science and history
tended to become civics or social studies with a primary emphasis on adjustment to current social norms rather than to
permanent natural or divine norms. Education had been re-
vised to turn out citizens with cooperative attitudes and
lightly held beliefs.

This brief review of some of the effects of the rise of a
pervasive attitude of scientific questioning and skepticism
suggests that these early years of the twentieth century may
have been one of the major periods of challenge to traditional
values. However this proposition may be judged of the
Western World in general, there seems little doubt about
the magnitude of the change in the United States. The
middle- and upper-class generations born after 1910 found
themselves surrounded by the rubble of once imposing structures of ordained truth. This alteration of the coordinates in
which the highly educated individual saw the mystery of his
relations to the world and the universe, whether in family
life, learning, religion, or social values, was a change com-
parable to that from the Middle Ages to the early modern
period, but very much more rapid.

7

Social Welfare

Government in every industrialized nation has been challenged by the need to preserve minimum standards of health, education, and security against extreme hardship. All this may be classed as social welfare. During more than two hundred years since the American Revolution the nature of these demands in all the Western nations has been continually changing. In addition to commonly shared problems, however, the United States has had those generated by taking in millions of immigrants as well as by the heritage of a small but unassimilated native population and of black slavery.

The Traditional View of Poverty

In America, at least, rural poverty in the eighteenth century was hard to measure. Records of land tilled by tenants or heavily mortgaged farmers even in the prosperous Middle States suggest a large degree of near poverty, undermaintenance, and debt.[1] With the rise of relatively large Colonial cities there was no question about the continuous existence of urban poverty. John K. Alexander, writing of eighteenth-century Philadelphia, estimates the poor at 10 percent of the population. But this could be divided between those who could not earn a living for reasons of age or ability and those like common sailors and other "laborers" who varied between employment, jail for disorderly conduct, and some form of relief.[2]

Well-to-do citizens regarded the poor, except for the physically disabled, as showing the results of improvident, misspent lives. This attitude, strongly entrenched in the Colonial period, made economic success a sign of virtue and poverty an early sign of the predestination to be damned, a rationalization that recalls Horace Mann's complaint: "In this country we seem to learn our rights quicker than our duties."[3]

Continuous waves of immigrants and movement within the country, together with seasonal layoffs, particularly in agriculture and in manufacturing that used waterpower, led to many temporary poor. To save the improvident among these potentially useful workers, cities distributed firewood, food, and clothing paid for by public funds or private charity.[4] The frequency of default on debts also attests to the insecurity of early employment: "The crude and imperfect evidence of the late eighteenth century suggests that as many as one householder in three may each year have been hauled into court as defaulting debtor."[5]

In spite of the increasing need of rapidly growing urban populations, both the relative amount and types of poor relief probably declined during the nineteenth century. The major cities undertook the study of poverty in the 1820s and generally decided to stop home relief and concentrate the poor in almshouses.[6] To an upper-income committee of investigation in Philadelphia, poverty seemed chiefly the result of intemperance. These practices and attitudes stretching well into the twentieth century represent the reenforcement of the strong cultural belief or value that poverty and sin were generally associated.

By the late nineteenth century some liberals were beginning to believe that unemployment resulting from severe depressions, such as those of 1873-1879 and 1893-1897, was not the fault of the workers, but the fact that among the unemployed there were likely to be many new immigrants and unskilled workers of ethnic backgrounds made it easier to blame their plight on not having "Americanized" themselves with sufficient diligence. The relatively more stable employment of the years from 1897 to 1930 took the interest of reformers away from the problems. The federal government, for example, kept no statistics on unemployment.

An unavoidable challenge to the old concepts of worker responsibility for idleness came from the magnitude of unemployment in the United States by early 1933. Even staunch upholders of the old values had reluctantly to recognize that it was unlikely that a quarter to a third of all workers were personally to blame for being unemployed. The shift of relief payments to the federal government in 1933 and the Social Security Act of 1935 marked a practical concession to social, as against the old personal, responsibility, but the administration instituted no study of poverty as such.[7]

Similarly, the Full Employment Act of 1946 could be said to mark another partial political defeat of the old moral value or ethic and the acceptance by a majority in Congress, although not quite rationally, of public responsibility for minimum standards of welfare. But the act was much more a gesture than a real change in policy. Even the greater interest in welfare introduced by Lyndon Johnson in 1964 failed to lead to any comprehensive national policies respecting unemployment and poverty. The conservatives of the 1980s still held to the pre-1930 values and saw welfare for the unemployed as an irksome cost, not as a problem needing creative solutions.

Education and Welfare

In only a few states of the early nineteenth century, perhaps only in Connecticut and Massachusetts, was general public education regarded as a desirable type of expenditure for tax money. By 1840 probably about half the children of New England were receiving free education, but perhaps only a seventh of those in the Middle States and still fewer in the South and West. Private schools existed in all areas, but enrolled only 10 to 20 percent of the children.[8]

The strongest force in perpetuating an educated population was the family household. Literate parents raised literate children, and semiliterate parents passed on their ignorance. Although literacy was essential to some jobs, a recent study of three Canadian counties in the early nineteenth century suggests that literacy did not guarantee jobs or success.[9] As noted earlier, the classic argument for free education by those approving of it was that it would promote the social welfare by teaching respect for, and obedience to, the status quo, not that it was needed for business or personal life.

A swing in business opinion toward favoring free elementary education began in the early 1830s and led to laws that permitted urban areas to use tax money for schools. The writings of Horace Mann of Massachusetts gave major impetus to this movement. It is said that by 1850 the United States was a world leader in primary education, but without laws compelling attendance, the real time spent by children in free schools is uncertain.

Effective challenges to a laissez-faire attitude toward public education came in the late nineteenth and early twentieth centuries from the increasing number of poorly educated urban immigrants and the rise of paperwork in business. Such considerations led, first in the old industrial areas and later in the South, to wider advocacy of elementary education. Between 1885 and 1915 most states passed compulsory school laws requiring attendance for so many days a year by children of certain ages. One may take the view that this need for more education was not a challenge to American values, but rather to American habits. Also, the American response was not widely different from that of the nations of northwestern Europe. As industrialism advanced, elementary education appeared necessary. Yet it represented perhaps the most important extension of government power in American history, one based on the inability of private educational enterprise and a laissez-faire attitude to produce satisfactory results.

The nineteenth-century spread of college education in small sectarian institutions in the United States was not primarily based on social or national welfare. Rather, it was a joint product of religious expansion and local boosterism.[10] Each sect wanted its own college, and if the faculty were as many as three, one member was very likely to have a doctrinal dispute with colleagues and start a new enterprise. A good-sized college was an important benefit to the merchants of a town and was worth moderate financial aid.

As seen in Chapter 6, this competitive college and university system in the United States responded to the need for management study more rapidly than in the nationally controlled systems of Europe. In the 1950s and 1960s, the presumed needs of industry, stimulated by fear of Russian technological advances, made both secondary and higher education appear necessary to the general welfare and resulted in the United States's leading the world in the percentage of its population in colleges that were increasingly state- or community-financed institutions. Again, as in lower education, the earlier value placed on private enterprise and responsibility was being challenged by the forces of change.

The Challenges of Immigration and Migration

In normal peacetime, caring for immigrants has seldom been regarded as a legitimate responsibility of the host nation. Even when Irish authorities in the 1840s paid for passage to America in order to get rid of starving people, no agreements were made with the states to care for or distribute the émigrés. Many migrants had come in the Colonial period under indenture requiring the signer to work for the purchaser of the note; and some, in later days under contract to an agent or employer. In the early nineteenth century, E. P. du Pont, for example, procured most of his Irish employees by special contracts.[11] Around the Middle States cities, a large fraction of the growing labor force was made up of immigrants. Temporarily checked by European wars, the stream rose to from 20,000 to 30,000 annually from 1815 to 1845 and then, because of bad harvests in Europe and railroad building in America, to a height of 600,000 by 1854.[12] This flood meant that a majority of welfare seekers in the northeastern ports were immigrants. Yet the fact that immigrants continued to come, even if they had to live in shacks at the edge of the cities, indicated hope for eventual success. Up until the quota acts of the 1920s, a large part of the indigents were recent immigrants. This helped to condition the older Americans against placing a positive value on responsibility for the poor and needy.

Furthermore, as the waves of immigration rose higher from 1880 to 1914, the large numbers of new immigrants seeking work were also resented by those who already had jobs, while the newcomers continued to be looked down upon by native-born Americans. The whole complex undoubtedly contributed to the continuing dissociation of middle-class Americans from the problem of the poor in both sustenance and housing.

In a minor way, the same complex worked in the new towns and cities of the West. Newcomers reaching out for opportunities might help to build up the town, but they also menaced the jobs of the insecure; and when, in addition, the newcomers were of a different nationality, resentments could be strong. The native-born New Englanders in the small lakeshore city of Milwaukee in the mid-nineteenth century, for example, resented the German immigrants, not only as competitors, but for their differing national customs, such as enjoying beer gardens and concert halls.[13]

Adjustment to American values by different racial or national groups has, of course, involved widely different problems. Germans, Scandinavians, and people from all the British Isles were usually absorbed into the majority culture. With these and other people of somewhat similar "Nordic," Anglo-Saxon, and Celtic origins, the "melting pot" seemed to work within a generation or two. With the southern and eastern European Christians, the process was slower. With Jews from the same areas, there was a two-way problem as the immigrants resisted assimilation. With black Africans, the majority values of the traditional American culture held assimilation to be undesirable. In the process of assimilation, the American Indians occupied a special place. Regarded by both Indians and whites as members of cultures that could not readily be mixed, the former were segregated on reservations. As Indian lands have been invaded and reduced in the twentieth century, many abler members of the tribes have joined white society. Here, in spite of theoretical respect for their ancient American heritage, they have often been victims of the color line.

Volumes have been written on these subjects. The points to be made here are the facts that, because of forced and voluntary immigration, inherited cultural values regarding ethnicity have been more continuously challenged here in America than in the other large Western nations and that neither in America nor abroad has there been a satisfactory regard for the welfare of minorities diverging widely in color or religion.

American blacks in the twentieth century may have benefited from going North to fill jobs during times of prosperity, particularly after immigration was checked and during the labor shortages of World Wars I and II, but in both North and South adverse discrimination continued in schooling and types of work. This was also true in the armed forces, which more or less subtly but effectively kept blacks in inferior positions. The problem represented a vicious circle. Blacks were less educated than whites, because of both inferior schools and economic handicaps. Consequently, they were less well prepared for jobs requiring relatively high levels of skill or learning, and keeping blacks at lower-income levels hindered their getting superior education for their children. Before the 1960s, blacks were also denied admission to many trade unions.

In the upsurge of thought about welfare and equality that started with the decision by the Supreme Court in *Brown* v. *Board of Education of Topeka* in 1954, holding that separate schools for blacks were manifestly discriminatory, through the Civil Rights acts of 1964 and 1965, which sought to protect voting rights and equality of opportunity in employment, blacks gained theoretical democracy and equality. On the surface, these values had been safeguarded, but did the words still have the same meaning? Southern whites like Thomas Jefferson proclaimed freedom, democray, and equality of opportunity, but still held slaves. Obviously, each word had qualifications. Freedom for or from what? Opportunity equal in what respects? Such examples emphasize the wide differences in inner meaning expressed by the same words and suggest a more general or holistic view of cultural values based on what the elite groups want to achieve or perpetuate. It was a splintering of such groups and a confusion of values in the face of new social situations that led to a temporarily liberal Supreme Court and Congress.

Welfare on the Job

Better physical conditions of work seem seldom to have been valued by employers before 1900. George Pullman and a few others built what they considered to be model factory towns, but gave little attention to conditions in the plant itself. In the new century men like Frederick W. Taylor called attention to the possibility of higher productivity from better working conditions. Although unions distrusted Taylor's "scientific" management, they approved of physically improving the plants in which their members worked. The progressive drive for workers' compensation for accidents and high rates of labor turnover in the relatively prosperous years from 1897 to 1912 also produced a rise of interest in the conditions of the workplace. The resulting improvements are usually lumped together under the slogan of "welfare capitalism." By 1910 outside consultants had convinced a number of employers that good lighting, fresh air, lockers, rest rooms, and showers paid off in better productivity. An increasing incentive to productivity was also sought through pay on the basis of piecework or shares in some measured amount of product. Another aspect of the movement was to attach workers to the welfare of the company by facilitating stock purchases and, in a very few instances, by pensions.

The effectiveness of all these plans based on the old values of rewarding individual initiative was dubious. Incentive pay for more work tended to be self-defeating when employers continually lowered the rates. Stock purchases and pension plans were defeated by the trouble they were supposed to help correct: labor turnover. Moreover, the small amount of stock a worker could afford to buy and the uncertainties of the market made such ownership seem of little importance.

There were, of course, exceptions to all these statements, usually in the case of medium-sized companies with active, liberal proprietors such as Henry F. Denison. But, by 1929, "welfare capitalism" no longer seemed a sufficient answer to labor unrest. Professor Elton Mayo of the Harvard Business School had reached the conclusion that the personal relations between labor managers and employees were more important than bonuses or other welfare devices.[14] The Mayo findings implying that in mechanized industry management was probably more responsible for high productivity than were workers was to have great long-run consequences. Even in service enterprise, good performance probably depends more on managerial arrangements than on the average ability of employees. The true force of this challenge was only to be realized during succeeding generations.[15]

Environmental Welfare

The values placed on freedom of enterprise and on rewarding the active operator had a long history in American law.[16] Entrepreneurs wishing to dam rivers for millraces had been upheld by the courts in the early nineteenth century against the complaints of farmers downstream. Similarly, a reflection of the value placed on the active exploiter is that little was done before the 1890s to conserve or regulate the use of timber and mineral resources in the West. Only the nearly intolerable conditions of soft coal smoke in early twentieth-century cities finally led to some clean air ordinances.

After World War I, new and insidious menaces to the quality of the physical environment came from the spread of the automobile and the rapid rise of the chemical industry. Automobiles gradually came under state regulations designed to increase safety in operation and then under federal laws from 1965 on to protect the air from excessive emissions of carbon monoxide.

The problems created by chemicals were more complex. Between 1930 and 1970, chemical production increased seven-fold, and its wastes or unwanted by-products might menace workers in plants and all people in surrounding areas, or the products might harm consumers. In general, such problems could only be dealt with effectively by the federal government, and precedents for action had been provided in the Food and Drug acts of 1906 and 1907. At this time some of the larger producers saw advantages in preventing the use of harmful preservatives or narcotics by small competitors. These early bills had the support of a committee of the National Association of Manufacturers, and there was relatively little business opposition to this restriction of freedom of enterprise in the name of social welfare.

The growing problems of contamination in the 1960s produced new action at the end of the decade, when Congress during the Nixon administration passed several laws and set up the Environmental Protection Agency. That the laws of 1906 and 1907 and those of 1968 to 1971 were passed by Republican administrations shows the general agreement that the value placed on freedom of enterprise had to be modified to fit that placed on public health.

The Welfare of Women

The very gradual shift in cultural values by a growing number of Americans from valuing women for their devotion to childbearing and rearing and maintenance of an adequate home to admitting that women's welfare demanded equality with men politically, socially, and economically is far too intricate a topic both psychologically and historically for this brief survey. Gains in equality of status have been periodic and at times transitory. In Colonial times, for example, widows frequently continued their husbands' businesses. In later days of more complex and larger operations carried on outside the home, female management was less likely. In the new American state constitutions of the late eighteenth century, women were usually not specifically denied political and legal rights, but the courts soon took these from them. The mid-nineteenth century agitation for equality led by Susan B. Anthony, Amelia Bloomer, Lucretia Mott, Lucy Stone, Elizabeth Cady Stanton, and others created a good deal of news; but except for their share in the abolition of slavery, some state temperance acts, and liberalization of the laws regarding property holdings, they accomplished relatively little.

In the late nineteenth century, women's gains in implementing the cultural value of "equality" were largely political and legal rather than economic or social. State laws were more often interpreted to allow women to control property apart from their husbands, to be trustees or guardians, and, in a few instances, chiefly in the West, to vote in local, territorial, or state elections. But the general cultural values still regarded women as custodians of home and family. In general, possibilities of employment were low-level, and work outside the home was disapproved of in the case of married women of middle-income families.

One might expect that the Progressive Movement and World War I would have brought a great expansion in the conceptions of female welfare, but, except for suffrage, this was not the case. The Nineteenth Amendment, passed in 1920, gave women equal voting rights with men, but because women were not active participants in managing the business or political worlds, the vote per se made little difference. Even in the field of higher education, one of the major areas of expansion in the 1920s, women continued to be discriminated against. Leading law and medical schools either excluded women altogether or held them to small quotas. College and university posts, save in schools of education, were extremely hard for women to obtain. In business and industry those jobs open to women paid them less than two-thirds of the male levels.[17]

The New Deal extended a number of potential opportunities to women and protected them from open discrimination, but because new jobs scarcely existed, little real progress in employment was achieved. The welfare of women in relation to rights and jobs was, in fact, about the same in 1940 as in 1920.

The upsurge in both status and employment for women, as well as for qualified blacks, started with World War II. First the war led to maximum employment, and when it was over, two decades of relative prosperity helped to perpetuate some of the wartime invasion of previously white male occupations. The congressional legislation of Lyndon Johnson's "Great Society" period seemed to ensure blacks their voting rights and both women and members of ethnic groups equal opportunities for jobs and education. These "equalities" involved more problems than can be discussed here, but they, at least, established trends that challenged the traditional values regarding the proper roles of women in society, a

challenge not confined to the United States and one promising continuous reappraisals.

Changing Problems in Social Welfare

The traditional American approaches to social problems have
emphasized individuals and what has appeared to be "common sense" or simple answers. The problems threatening the
welfare of society by the 1980s involve millions of people and
very rapidly growing technological and scientific knowledge.
Social welfare should ultimately be guided by new demo-
graphic, technological, and scientific findings of the late twentieth century. Such aids as may be found may not necessarily
contradict the older values, but any congruance will likely
be accidental.

8

Challenges of the 1980s

All the industrialized cultures have faced many of the same challenges in the twentieth century, but, because of varying national heritages and experiences, the challenged values have differed. Wars, dictatorships, growth, and depression have occurred differently in each region. For example, although the United States was not in the forefront in growth in income per capita, having started from a higher level in the mid-nineteenth century, with values in harmony with rising production and consumption, it developed the culture with the most "middle-class" values. Starting as a democracy, the United States had equalitarian values that were not seriously challenged by new forces. In extreme contrast to the United States, Japan in 1850 was still feudal and agricultural and at the end of the century was just entering the modern industrial world. Japan's "vertical" society of superiority and deference, of group activity with strong attachments to employers and localities differed in almost every important respect from the United States' "horizontal," democratic, individualistic, and migratory society. In Japan a "horizontal" approach of free give-and-take between business associates was unpleasant and virtually impossible except among trusted friends. Democracy and social equality have, therefore, represented much greater challenges to Japanese values than to those of the United States.

An Era of Confidence

The totality of the challenges that emerged or grew in the twentieth century seems more dramatic in view of the self-confidence of the old order in the America of 1900. According to Henry F. May, the nineteenth-century American heritage included "the reality, certainty and eternity of moral values" and a strong belief in progress.[1] The nations of northwestern Europe also faced the twentieth century from high points of self-assurance. Between them they unquestionably controlled the world, and the nineteenth-century European achievements in all the arts and sciences had created a truly great civilization. Although Americans had made relatively small contributions to science and the arts, their equally advanced technology, mass production, and newly acquired naval power led them to share in the Western euphoria. In the oft-quoted words of Herbert Croly in 1909: "They still believe that somehow and sometime something better will happen to good Americans than has happened to men in any other country,"[2] Teddy Roosevelt portrayed his militant type of Americanism as a powerful "moral" force, American steel began to sell competitively in the world market, American missionaries hoped to Christianize Asia, and only in America could middle-income people afford automobiles. In addition, except to a handful of scholars of world affairs, permanent peace, other than "police action" by the great powers, seemed possible to people in the United States.

These confident years of the early century produced a belief in an Anglo-Saxon duty to "civilize" and Christianize the "heathen" nations. Senator Albert J. Beveridge said: "God has not been preparing the English-speaking and Teutonic peoples for a thousand years for nothing but vain and idle self-contemplation. He has marked the American people as His chosen nation to finally lead in the regeneration of the world."[3] This sense of mission was, no doubt, stronger among the upper classes than among the lower ones, but, being a gratifying belief, it appears to have been widespread in America. Somewhat similar chauvinism appeared in England, France, and Germany.

As all deep cultural change is slow and the early twentieth century represented a flowering of many of the values and drives of the historic culture, it is not surprising that the same values and attitudes persisted in the United States through World War I and the relatively untroubled 1920s. Furthermore, contradictory values may exist side by side for long periods. For Europe, World War I was a traumatic experience that disturbed and cast doubt on basic values of the nineteenth-century culture, whereas in the United States the effect was, in part, a superficial reenforcement of the feeling of American world supremacy. As late as 1960, a diverse group of leading and probably representative American intellectuals such as Robert Hutchins, Henry Luce, Thornton Wilder, and Jacques Barzun were held to exemplify "a culture built on rigorous moral discipline, social responsibility, a reverence for work, and a respect for psychic restraint"—the historic values of the American elite.[4]

Challenges to Democracy

From the seventeenth to the nineteenth centuries, the fundamental American values of democracy and self-determination had been nurtured in small local societies with large participation in elections by those eligible to vote. As organized activity, whether private or public, grew larger; autocratic control from above became increasingly the rule. This raised a continuing question of whether democratic values could keep their strength when a third to a half of the qualified adults did not bother to vote and when the average employee of either government or business was not governed by such values in practice. In civilian government, democracy existed in theory, at least; in business bureaucracy, democracy existed no more than it did in the growing military sphere.

When Charles Percy of Illinois left the top executive group of a large corporation to become a United States senator, he said: "It's a terrible plunge into an icy bath to jump from business, which is essentially an autocracy, into government, which is a democracy."[5] At his level, at least, the bath was democratic. In business, Andrew Carnegie's advice to young men to "boss your boss" was beyond the realm of possibility in a well-ordered, big company hierarchy. That democracy, the most celebrated and sacred cluster of American values, would survive in individual emotions seemed probable, but that such values would have to be put on a shelf during part of the day by those who worked in bureaucracies seemed certain.[6]

Also challenging to democracy was the continued antagonism between business and representative government. Here the existing adversary relations between entrepreneurs and the wealthy on one side and all levels of government on the other continued. The negative value placed on government, particularly accentuated in the late nineteenth century, continued even though federal agencies became the best customers of many big businesses. As the mayor of Minneapolis said: "We have not yet evolved in America an understandable and acceptable role or status for the politician."[7] And he might have added: "or any government employees." As emphasized in Chapter 7, Americans had never had a strong feeling of duty to the state or put a value on service to the state as the most prestigious of occupations. In part, this came from the relative lack of foreign menaces to the nation from 1815 to the rise of Hitler, but it also seems that continual migration had weakened loyalty to places, people, and institutions.

In spite of the utility of the federal government to much of big business, nonmilitary federal expenditures were feared and resisted more than such expenditures by state and local governments. A factor in favoring the latter agencies was the fact that when, exceeding their revenue, they borrowed by

means of tax-exempt bonds, an attractive investment to those
paying high taxes whereas federal bonds and Treasury notes
were fully subject to the graduated national income tax. Furthermore, the borrowing and spending abilities of the state
and local agencies were in many ways limited by competition
between localities whereas borrowing by the federal government had no constraints. Hence the United States responded
relatively inefficiently to the challenge of using central government to meet the ever-changing needs of an industrial
nation.

But in spite of any possible new efficiencies in bureaucratic
structure, the federal government and the central authority
in other large nations, as well as in some private corporations,
raised the problem of the limits of governability. How big
and how many-tiered could a hierarchy be and still function
with reasonable honesty and efficiency? Obviously, there is
no uniform answer. Efficiency depends in large part on the
cultural motivations of the servants of bureaucracy. Yet no
large organization can escape the problem or confidently
deny that there are diminishing returns to increasing size.
The late J. Howard Pew, major power in the Sun Oil company, said to the Temporary National Committee in 1939:
"I very definitely believe that there is in every corporation
the seeds of destruction, and that inevitably when a corporation gets too large it is going to go broke."[8] A national state
cannot "go broke" in the same sense, but it may become less
governable because of size and organization.

Other Challenges to Individual Choice and Action

As seen in Chapter 7, the automobile and chemical industries
forced regulations to protect public health from toxic wastes
and air pollution. As a result, there was more new federal
regulation from 1969 to 1972 by a Republican government
than had occurred in any equal time since the days of the
New Deal. The Arab oil embargo of 1973-1974 added a new

pressure for regulations to conserve energy and for appropriations to grant government assistance to energy studies.

The situation and its remedies went counter to an implicit but unjustified belief in the endless resources of the continent. Though some minerals had been in short supply for many decades, the assumption had persisted that substitutes could be found when needed. Suddenly to run short of the developed forms of energy because of the activities of foreigners challenged the American values placed on progress and self-sufficiency to a greater degree than any previous shortage. The long distances and extreme climates of the United States on the one hand made demand for energy relatively greater than in Western Europe or Japan, but on the other hand, North America still had great unexplored natural resources.

Pressure against any existing values are likely to be blamed on what may be called scapegoat factors. One of these is that by the mid-twentieth century a Calvinistic "work ethic" was somehow lost because of the effect on workers in manufacturing of the growth of unions and big company labor contracts. Yet analysts of earlier productivity fail to find unusually diligent work. Daniel T. Rodgers, in a recent book on the "work ethic" in earlier times, concludes: "It was not the pace of work in America . . . so much as its universality, its bewilderingly exalted status, the force of the idea itself."[9] In other words, the work ethic was a cultural value—not necessarily at any time an economic reality.

In some respects, World War II and its aftermath again reenforced an equally mythical image of America as God's chosen country and of American values of initiative, action, and self-help as superior to those of other nations. American troops in World War II were reported as performing miracles of military construction, while the demolition of much of the industrialized world's capital equipment provided an unusual postwar market for American technology. From 1948 on, this market was held partly by federal subsidies in the form of foreign aid that required purchases in the United States or, in other words, by government-subsidized exports.[10] By the 1980s, just as in the past, the United States again faced some superior technology in other nations, but the brief period of leadership in new developments from 1946 to about 1960 had given some American manufacturers a false sense of security and reduced their relative expenditure for research.

An inescapable technological challenge to older American habits and values, becoming increasingly obvious in the 1980s, was a shift away from employment in manufacturing. As technology improved throughout the twentieth century, the most advanced nations needed relatively fewer employees in production and more in the service areas of the economy. In the 1970s two new developments were speeding this change: automation in domestic manufacturing and fabrication of intricate handcrafted components in countries with cheap labor. Adding to the diminution in the need for male labor in domestic production was the rapid increase of women in the work force. In fact, total employment per capita established high records in the 1970s and early 1980s at the same time that "unemployment" was increasing. In 1982 women made up 48 percent of the labor force.[11] A palliative for unemployment not used anywhere in the industrial world was the old Utopian idea of the greatly shorter workday. Transition to such a system would have to be planned, and neither employed workers nor employers wanted it—the workers because they would probably lose pay; employers because it would complicate supervision and scheduling.

The combination of these factors affecting employment and the effects of slower growth in population from 1960 on, meaning fewer new households in the 1980s, were challenging the traditional values regarding individual economic responsibilities. It was no longer clear that even in good times the business system, if left to itself, could provide a job for every able and willing worker. Too many of the possibili-

ties of more work were in education, public improvements of
many types, and health services, none of which lent themselves to the American value of working for profit. Also, the
new jobs coming in information and other skilled services required special training for which the poorly educated adult
could not qualify.

The concept of the society as an interrelated whole, too
complex to rely on "the free market" for goods and service
as its guide, was the most fundamental challenge to American values concerning individual responsibility and the virtues of competition. Consequently, moves toward planning
of any sort were resisted by most of those in the population
who were succeeding well in the existing system. Although
poverty was grudgingly recognized as a continuing social
problem, no efforts to design a social system for its minimiza-
tion, a monumental task, were publicly initiated.[12] It was a
problem that was bound to grow and change with shifts in
the types of jobs generated by unplanned developments in
the economy and, therefore, was a fundamental challenge to
American individualistic values.

Challenges to Moral Belief

In essence, the failure squarely to face the problem of unemployment and poverty involved deep moral values, but ones
not generally associated with spiritual belief. The traditional
values of the latter, however, also suffered from new challenges in the mid-twentieth century. Although in the earlier
years of the century biblical criticism, evolution, relativity,
and subatomic physics were shown to have been accompanied
by a rise in religious skepticism among the highly educated,
the groups immediately involved were then relatively small.
The relentless challenge of science to all traditional belief,
however, steadily increased. In the late 1930s, new ideas
about the possible nature of ultimate or "unconditional"
power in the universe that would be more in tune with cur-

rent learning began to reach the United States, both from the writings of men like Dietrich Bonhoeffer and Paul Tillich of Germany and from the migration of the latter to Harvard University. Called by some neoorthodoxy, the doctrine held that God was not someone up in Heaven, but rather "the depth of being" within ourselves. Although Bonhoeffer was executed by the Nazis in 1944, his views spread in the 1950s and 1960s. The denial of a God in Heaven in place of a spiritual force deep in the individual led to the slogan "God is dead," which quite misrepresented the new doctrine. The new ideas put strong emphasis on Christ as embodying a divine message to humankind; Tillich called himself a Christologist, but denied the infallibility of the Bible. The view that "the Kingdom of Heaven was within" was popularly argued by John A. T. Robinson, Episcopal Bishop of Woolwich in London, in a book entitled *Honest to God,* which went through many printings from 1963 on.

Because the largest denominations in the United States were churches that were not willing to question the biblical heritage or the image of an anthropomorphic God, the crusade to make a spiritual force believable to highly educated modern thinkers was widely regarded as a challenge to religion. The socially divisive effect was probably greater in the United States than in Europe because of the strength of American evangelical faith and its followers' strong reaction against new interpretations. But the less defined spiritual ideas inevitably challenged moral certainties that were among the oldest and strongest American values without offering something equally understandable. In the 1970s the prominent sociologist Daniel Bell thought: "The lack of a moral belief system is the cultural contradiction of the society, the deepest challenge to its survival.[13]

Whether the confusion in religious values, the sheer size of hierarchies such as large, impersonal bureaucratic structures, or other more subtle forces were responsible, the Western World in the period after 1960 suffered a weakening of long-accepted standards of sex and conduct.[14] To some extent, street violence and crime were stimulated by new mixings of ethnic groups such as East and West Indians in London and movements of blacks and Hispanics in the United States. Three eminent social analysts contended in 1981: ". . . what lies behind the loss of a sense of positive direction is the disappearance of the core of sacred beliefs which . . . have always been at the heart of any genuine culture. Our troubles stem from lack of belief in something greater than the life immediately around us . . . science erodes the older bases of moral legitimation and produces none of its own."[15]

The Future

In addition to all the pressures against older values that have impinged since the mid-nineteenth century, the emergence of fear of a rival military power, weak or absent from 1815 to 1940 and never strong before that, appears as one of the most immediately upsetting pressures. The Russian development of the atomic bomb in the 1950s ended a brief dream by some Americans of uncontested world supremacy. In its place came a fear of world destruction, but still an insistence that the United States must be supreme and assume the duty of protecting a "free world." The problem does not so much affect specific values—Americans have always been self-righteous and activist—as it casts a pall of fear of the end of the world over all other problems.

Regardless of large inconsistencies between cultural values and the need for adjustment to new environments, change has always been gradual. A commentator on early America notes that "more often than not, rather than faithfully reflecting social reality, ideals and values are at odds with it, inverted mirror images of society as it is."[16] Late twentieth-century Americans are no doubt making many unconscious adjustments toward accepting the new values that need to be placed on contemplation, abstract knowledge, and the governmental provision of planning and services not profitable or affordable on a market basis. But such change need not prevent the continued placing of a high value on activity, competition, or personal success. The changes, however, may alter the meaning of these values from monetary triumphs in the market to those of a rewarding career or "fame" from some special achievement.

Each generation will inevitably move somewhat toward accepting the values of emerging orders and believing less devoutly in those of the traditional heritage. David M. Potter held that the United States was often a step ahead in actual social change and a step behind in its recognition. At all events, beliefs must always be seen in what Kenneth Burke calls a strategic context; that is, they can't be too much or too long in conflict with the dominant forces of the environment.

Notes

1   HISTORY AND VALUES

1. David Mandel, *Changing Art Changing Man*. See also writings by Gabriel Almond, Daniel Bell, Marvin Chodoric, Seymour Lipsett, Robert Nisbet, and many other social scientists.
2. Robin M. Williams, Jr., "Individual and Group Values," *Annals of the American Academy of Political and Social Science*, 371 (May 1967), 26.
3. See Harvard University Program on Technology and Society, *Technology and Values*, Research Review, No. 3, Summer 1969.
4. In earlier essays I used certain manifestations of culture such as "modal personalities" and "social roles" to explain consistencies in American history. Experience has suggested that though these concepts are fuller and more precise as explanations of how culture is actually manifested in behavior, they introduce a host of definitions and delicate differentiations that are not essential to seeing the broad outlines of how cultural values, geography, and society interact to produce or inhibit change. For more on culture, see Anthony F. C. Wallace, *Culture and Personality*; Ward H. Goodenough, *Description and Comparison in Cultural Anthropology*; and Clifford Geertz, "The Way We Think Now: Toward an Ethnography of Modern Thought," *Bulletin of the American Academy of Arts and Science*, 35 (February 1982).

5. Talcott Parsons, "Culture and Social Systems Revisited," in Louis Schneider and Charles Bonjean, eds., *The Idea of Culture in the Social Sciences,* p. 35.
6. See Steve Feldman, "The Career Culture of Management," M.S. thesis, University of Pennsylvania, 1983.
7. See H. G. Barnett, *Innovation: The Basis of Cultural Change.*
8. Everitt S. Lee, "The Turner Thesis Reexamined," *American Quarterly* 13 (Spring 1961).
9. Merle E. Curti et al., *The Making of an American Community.*
10. Sidney Goldstein, ed., *The Norristown Study,* pp. 89-91.

2 THE COLONIAL HERITAGE

1. *Democracy in America,* I, p. 33. See also Morton White, *Pragmatism and the American Mind,* pp. 3-4.
2. *Mechanization Takes Command: A Contribution to History,* p. 39.
3. Daniel Boorstin, *The Exploring Spirit,* p. 23.
4. See James A. Henretta, "Families and Forms: Mentalité in Pre-Industrial America," *Williams and Mary Quarterly,* 35 (January 1978), 3-32.
5. Quoted from Joyce Appleby, "Commercial Farming and the Agrarian Myth in the Early Republic," *Journal of American History,* 68 (March 1982), 844.
6. Winthrop S. Hudson, *Religion in America,* p. 12.
7. Mark A. Noll, "From the Great Awakening to the War of Independence: Christian Values in the American Revolution," *Christian Scholars Review,* 12 (1983), 104.
8. Winthrop S. Hudson, *Religion in America,* p. 30.
9. Thomas C. Cochran, *Business in American Life,* pp. 38-39.
10. Quoted in Victor S. Clark, *History of Manufactures in the United States, 1607-1860,* p. 211.
11. Edwin J. Perkins, *The Economy of Colonial America,* p. 145.
12. See Michael Zuckerman, "Fate, Flux, and Good Fellowship: An Early Virginia Design for the Dilemma of American Business," in Harold I. Sharlin, ed., *Business and Its Environment: Essays for Thomas C. Cochran.*
13. George E. Littlefield, *Early Schools and Schoolbooks of New England,* p. 114.

14. Perkins, *Economy of Colonial America,* p. 128.
15. John K. Alexander, *Render Them Submissive,* p. 19.

3 OLD VALUES REENFORCED

1. Watt's engine was little used in the United States, and in 1800 only a quarter of the steam engines in Britain were of Watt's design, and none were high pressure. John Fitch and Henry Voight designed advanced types of double acting, condensing engines for their steamboats without ever having seen a Watt type of steam engine.
2. See Donald R. Adams, "The Mid-Atlantic Labor Market in the Early Nineteenth Century," *In Business and Economic History: Papers Presented at the Twenty-fourth Annual Meeting of the Business History Conference,* 1979.
3. Henry Adams, *Writings of Albert Gallatin,* I, p. 653.
4. Quoted from George E. Probst, *The Happy Republic: A Reader in Tocqueville's America 7-8.* See also T. R. Winnpenny, "Cultural Factors in the Persistence of Hand Technology in Lancaster, Pennsylvania," *Pennsylvania History,* 50 (July 1983), 218-228.
5. See for example, Joseph S. Davis, *Essays in the Early History of American Corporations,* and George S. Gibb, *The Whitesmiths of Taunton.*
6. See various factory payrolls for 1800 to 1850 at the Eleutherian Mills Historical Library; also Anthony F. C. Wallace, *Rockdale.*
7. See Murray G. Murphey, "An Approach to the Study of National Character," in Milford Spero, ed., *Meaning and Content in Cultural Anthropology,* p. 141.
8. For more, see Cochran, *Business in American Life,* pp. 95 ff.
9. Harvey C. Minnich, *Old Favorites from the McGuffey Readers.*
10. For a contrary view, that the slave owners acted as businesspeople, see James Oakes, *A History of American Slaveholders,* and Michael Zuckerman, "Fate, Flux, and Good Fellowship: An Early Virginia Design for the Dilemma of American Business," in H. I. Sharlin, ed., *Business and Its Environment,* pp. 6-184.
11. Richard B. Morris, *Studies in the History of American Law,* p. 47.

12. Oscar Handlin and Mary Flug Handlin, *Commonwealth*, pp. 145-146.
13. See Tony A. Freyer, *Forums of Order*, pp. 53-98.
14. Peter J. Coleman, *Debtors and Creditors*, p. 285.
15. Becoming a county seat brought many lawyers and much business to a town.
16. *Democracy in America*, Vol. 1, p. 389.
17. I cannot agree with the popular importance of the Enlightenment implied in Henry Steel Commager's *The Empire of Reason*.
18. See Robert N. Bellah, "Civil Religion in America," *Daedalus* (Winter 1967), 1-21.
19. Charles V. Hagnar, *Early History of the Falls of the Schuykill, Manayunk, Schuykill and Lehigh Navigation Companies*, 33.
20. Michael Chevalier, quoted in George E. Probst et al. *The Happy Republic*, pp. 186-187.
21. Thomas Hamilton, *Men and Manners in America* (Edinburgh: 1843), p. 74.

4 GROWTH OF A NATION

1. "Fate, Flux and Good Fellowship = An Early Virginian Design for the Dilemma of American Business," in H. I. Sharlin, ed., *Business and Its Environment*, p. 164; see also James Oakes, *A History of American Slave-holders*, for the uniformities between slaveholders, and Northern capitalists' culture.
2. Jules Henry, *Culture Against Man*, p. 13.
3. Nathan Miller, *The Enterprise of a Free People*, p. 32.
4. *Works*, Autograph ed., ed. Richard Garnett (London, 1899), II, pp. 101-103.
5. For a discussion of the transfer of "belonging" to new types of community, see Daniel Boorstin, *The Americans*, v. 3.
6. I presented these ideas with more statistical detail in "The Paradox of American Economic Growth," *Journal of American History*, 61 (March, 1975), 925-942. The statistics are not good enough to make a reasonably exact comparison of real income per capita between Britain and the United States in 1850. Food and rent were cheaper in America, and because they are large items for the average citizen, I am inclined to put the United States ahead in average real satisfaction.

7. David Potter, *People of Plenty*. Americans were, to be sure, among the leading nations in income per capita, but were not unique. What Potter has correctly said was that the belief in unusual opportunity could replace the actuality. He wrote before the major statistical studies had appeared.

8. Robert E. Gallman, "Gross National Product in the United States, 1834-1909," in *Conference on Income and Wealth 8.* Also see Thomas C. Cochran, "The Paradox of Economic Growth," pp. 926-929; and Edward F. Denison, *Why Growth Rates Differ.*

9. See Cochran, "Paradox," p. 931 and footnotes. Next to the demand for small arms, the war's chief stimulating effect on the iron and steel industry was the demand for horseshoes.

10. Simon Kuznets, "Notes on the Pattern of U.S. Economic Growth," in R. W. Fogel and S. L. Engerman, eds., *The Reinterpretation of American Economic History*, pp. 18-19. If the U.S. growth were measured by major areas, large differences would be found.

11. "Late Nineteenth Century American Retardations: A Neoclassical Analysis," *Journal of Economic History*, 33 (September 1973) 592-593.

12. John W. Kendrick, *Productivity Trends in the United States*, pp. 333-340; and Kuznets, "Notes on the Pattern of U.S. Economic Growth," p. 21.

13. Historians of weather patterns now believe that the West was more arid in previous centuries than at present.

14. W. Paul Strassman, *Risk and Technological Innovation— American Manufacturing Methods During the 19th Century*, p. 221.

15. *Modern Economic Growth: Rate, Structure and Spread*, p. 491.

16. Roger Burlingame, *The American Conscience*, p. 206. See also William Warren Sweet, *Revivalism in America*, p. 118.

5 BUREAUCRACY

1. See Michael Kammen, ed., *The Contrapuntal Civilization: Essays Toward a New Understanding of the American Experience.*

2. See John A. Armstrong, *The European Administrative Elite.*

3. *Democracy in America,* II, p. 99.
4. See Paul W. Gates, "The Homestead Act in an Incongruous Land System," *American Historial Review,* 41 (July 1936), 652-681.
5. See James Bryce, *The American Commonwealth;* and Thomas C. Cochran, *Railroad Leaders.*
6. Review of Samuel P. Huntington, *American Politics: The Promise of Disharmony,* in *The New York Times Book Review,* November 15, 1981, p. 3.
7. Marvin Meyers, "Venturous Conservative," in Michael Kammen, ed., *The Contrapuntal Civilization,* p. 169.
8. Quoted from Thomas C. Cochran, *Railroad Leaders,* p. 82.
9. Jacob E. Price, *France and the Chesapeake,* I, pp. 116-126.
10. *The Empire of Business,* p. 192.
11. See Alfred D. Chandler, Jr., *Henry Varnum Poor.*
12. Alfred D. Chandler, Jr., "Henry Varnum Poor," in William Miller, ed., *Men in Business,* 256.
13. Ibid., p. 268.
14. See Irene D. Neu, *Erastus Corning.*
15. Chandler, *Poor,* p. 156.
16. Ibid., 265.
17. Ibid. In *The Visible Hand: The Managerial Revolution in American Business,* Part II, Chandler has ably described the evolution of railroad management.
18. *The Contrapuntal Civilization: Essays Toward a New Understanding of American Experience,* p. 26.
19. *Time Magazine,* May 27, 1981, p. 66.
20. See Thomas C. Cochran, *Railroad Leaders: The Business Mind in Action,* pp. 226 ff.
21. Ralph W. Hidy and Muriel Hidy, *Pioneering in Big Business 1882-1911: History of the Standard Oil Co., New Jersey,* Vol. 1, pp. 323-338.
22. Ibid., p. 329.
23. *The Human Problems of an Industrial Civilization.*
24. See Thomas C. Cochran, "The Sloan Report—American Culture and Business Management," *American Quarterly,* 27 (1975) 1-15.
25. See Alfred D. Chandler and Steven Salsbury, *Pierre S. Du Pont and the Making of the Modern Corporation.*

26. See J. Patrick Wright, *On A Clear Day You Can See General Motors.*

27. Yugoslavia has worker "control" through work councils in privately owned companies, but in general the councils lack the information necessary to direct policy. The addition of labor members to boards of directors in other European nations has done little either to bring democracy or to alleviate bureaucratic problems.

28. I will not enter into a discussion of apparently incurable problems of big organizations that are well treated in books such as Michel Crozier's *The Bureaucratic Phenomenon.* For example, the age-old maxim that decisions should be made at the lowest possible level contradicts the principle that subordinate behavior should, as far as possible, be predictable. See Steve Feldman, "The Career Culture of Management," Ph.D. dissertation, University of Pennsylvania, 1983.

29. J. Woodward, in Tom Burns, *Industrial Man,* p. 196. This generalization might not apply to a hundred or more giant companies in the United States that have highly structured systems. See Alfred D. Chandler, Jr., *Strategy and Structure— Chapters in the History of American Industrial Enterprise.*

30. Quoted in Eugene Staley, ed., *Creating an Industrial Civilization,* p. 62.

31. "How to Become a Railroad President," *What's New* (November 1949), p. 13.

32. Quoted in Paul W. Litchfield, *Industrial Voyage.*

33. Quoted in Herrymon Maurer, *Great Enterprise: Growth and Behavior of the Big Corporation,* p. 161.

34. See David Riesman, *The Lonely Crowd;* William H. Whyte, *The Organizational Man;* Robert V. Presthus, *The Organizational Society;* Ralph Hummel, *The Bureaucratic Experience.* It has been argued that women adapt to the demands of bureaucracy more readily than men.

35. Margaret Frenn, quoted by Suzanne Gordon in "The New Corporate Feminism," *The Nation,* February 5, 1983, p. 146.

6   THE CHALLENGE OF SCIENCE

1. See Harold I. Sharlin, *The Convergent Century: The Unification of Science in the Nineteenth Century.*

2. For an excellent discussion of this problem, see Charles Rosenberg, *No Other Gods: On Science and American Social Thought*. Richard Hofstadter provides a similar social approach in his *Anti-Intellectualism in American Life*.

3. See Minutes of the Academy on Microfilm, Scholarly Resources, Wilmington, Del.

4. *No Other Gods*, p. 205.

5. See David J. Pivar, *The American Purity League*.

6. Louis Filler, ed., *Horace Mann and the Crisis in Education*, pp. 8-9.

7. See, for example, Johannes Weiss, *Earliest Christianity: A History of the Period A.D. 30-150*.

8. The remainder of this chapter is taken to a large extent from Thomas C. Cochran, *The Inner Revolution*, Chapter 1.

9. *The New Age of Faith*, p. 18.

10. *The Mysterious Universe*, pp. 172 ff.

11. *Seven Psychologies*, 198.

12. John B. Watson, "Psychology as the Behaviorist Views it," *Psychological Review*, 20 (1913), 158-177. His most influential book was *Psychology from the Standpoint of a Behaviorist*. For new ideas about the brain, see Jeremy Campbell, *Grammatical Man: Information, Entropy, Language and Life;* and Charles J. Lumsden and Edward O. Wilson, *Promethean Fire: Reflections on the Origin of Mind*.

13. William E. Leuchtenburg, *The Perils of Prosperity*, p. 163.

14. Will Herberg, *Protestant, Catholic, Jew*, p. 31.

15. Mary Allen West, *Childhood: Its Care and Culture*. Miss West was a specialist who had studied children in "thousands of homes." For this and the following references, I am indebted to Rosamond Cochran for research on late nineteenth- and early twentieth-century educational and child-rearing writings.

16. *Conscious Motherhood*, p. 83. Emma Marwedel brought the ideas of Froebel to bear on child-rearing and education from 1871 on.

17. See, for example, Jacob Abbott, *Gentle Measures in the Management and Training of Children*: Julia McNair Wright, *Practical Life or Ways and Means for Developing Character and Resources;* Mary E. Sherwood, *Amenities at Home;* C. E.

Sargent, *Our Home or the Key to a Nobler Life;* and Reverend W. F. Crafts, *Childhood: The Text-Book of the Age of Parents, Pastors and Teachers.*

18. Geoffrey H. Steere, "Changing Values in Child Socialization: A Study of United States Child-Rearing Literature, 1865-1929." Unpublished Ph.D. dissertation, University of Pennsylvania, 1964.
19. Ibid., Chapter 4.
20. M. V. O'Shea, *First Steps in Child Training*, p. 25.
21. Ibid., p. 28.
22. Steere, "Child Socialization," Chapter 4.
23. Dewey, *Individualism Old and New*, p. 138.
24. "My Pedagogic Creed," in Oscar Handlin, ed., *John Dewey's Challenge to Education.*
25. Dewey, *Individualism Old and New*, p. 141.
26. See Lawrence A. Cremin, *The Transformation of the School*, p. 193.
27. See Raymond E. Calahan, *Education and the Cult of Efficiency.*

7 SOCIAL WELFARE

1. Jack Michel, "In a manner suitable to their degree: A preliminary investigation of the material culture of early Pennsylvania," *Working Papers from the Regional Economic History Research Center*, Vol. 5, No. 1 (1981), 1–83.
2. *Render Them Submissive;* and Billy G. Smith, "The Best Poor Man's Country: Living Standards of the Lower Sort in Late 18th century Philadelphia," *Working Papers from the Regional Economic History Research Center*, Vol. 2, No. 4 (1979), 1–70.
3. Louis Filler, ed., *Horace Mann and the Crisis in Education*, p. 5.
4. Gary Lawson Brown, *Baltimore in the Nation, 1789–1861*, p. 97. See also Billy G. Smith, "The Best Poor Man's Country . . ."
5. Peter J. Coleman, *Debtors and Creditors in America*, p. 287.
6. Priscilla Ferguson Clement, "The Philadelphia Welfare Crisis of the 1820s," *Pennsylvania Magazine of History and Biography*, 55 (April 1981), 153–158.

7. James T. Patterson, *America's Struggle Against Poverty, 1900–1980,* p. 75.

8. George W. Edwards and Herman G. Richey, *The School in the American Social Order,* p. 53.

9. See H. J. Graff, *The Literacy Myth: Literacy and Social Structure in the Nineteenth Century City.*

10. See Thomas C. Cochran, *Business in American Life,* pp. 98–99.

11. Harold Hancock, *The Industrial Worker Along the Brandywine, 1800–1830,* p. 15

12. *Historical Statistics of the United States,* p. 57.

13. See Thomas C. Cochran, *The Pabst Brewing Company.*

14. See Chapter 6.

15. See Reinhard Bendix, *Work and Authority in Industry.*

16. See Willard Hurst, *Law and Social Process in United States History.*

17. William Henry Chafe, *The American Woman—Her Changing Social, Economic and Political Roles, 1920–1970,* pp. 60 ff.

8 CHALLENGES OF THE 1980s

1. *The End of American Innocence,* pp. 9–10. See also Thomas C. Cochran, "The Social Scientists," in Robert E. Spiller and Eric Larrabee, eds., *American Perspectives,* pp. 94–98.

2. *The Promise of American Life,* p. 3.

3. Quoted from A. M. Schlesinger, Jr., "America: Experiment or Destiny?" *American Historical Review,* 81 (1976), 517.

4. James Sloan Allen, *The Romance of Commerce and Culture,* p. 291.

5. Quoted from Herrman E. Kroos, *Executive Opinion: What Business Leaders Said and Thought on Economic Issues, 1920–1960,* p. 252.

6. See Thomas C. Cochran, "History and Cultural Crisis," *American Historical Review,* 78 (1973).

7. Edward C. Banfield and James Q. Wilson, *City Politics,* p. 246.

8. Personal conversation with J. H. Pew. A half century earlier, William James wrote to a friend: "I am against bigness and greatness in all forms . . . the bigger the unit you deal with, the hollower, the more brutal, the more mendacious the life

displayed" (quoted from Morton White, *Pragmatism and the American Mind*, p. 20).

9. *The Work Ethic in Industrial America 1850–1920*, p. 6. See also Herbert Gutman, "Work, Culture and Society in Industrial America, 1815–1919," *American Historical Review*, 88 (1973), 532–587.

10. This practice was strongly denounced by those exporters who received none of the gains.

11. Business Week Work Team, *The Reindustrialization of America*, pp. 25 ff.

12. See James T. Patterson, *America's Struggle Against Poverty*.

13. *The Cultural Contradictions of Capitalism*, p. 481.

14. See Thomas C. Cochran, "History and Cultural Crisis," *American Historical Review*, 78 (February 1973).

15. Gabriel A. Almond, Marvin Chodorov, and Roy Harvey Pearce, "Progress and Its Discontents," *Bulletin of the American Academy of Arts and Sciences* 35 (1981), 12–13. David Mandel sees the same breakdown in belief clearly indicated by confusion in the arts in *Changing Art Changing Man*.

16. Christine Leigh Heyerman, "The Fashion Among More Superior People: Charity and Social Change in Provincial New England, 1700–1740," *American Quarterly*, 34 (1982), 124; and Morton White, *Pragmatism and the American Mind*, pp. 3–4.

Bibliography

Abbott, Jacob. *Gentle Measures in the Management and Training of Children.* New York: Harper, 1871.

Adams, Donald R. "The Mid-Atlantic Labor Market in the Early Nineteenth Century." In *Business and Economic History: Papers Presented at the Twenty-fourth Annual Meeting of the Business History Conference.* Greenwich, CT: JAI Press, 1979.

Adams, Henry. *Writings of Albert Gallatin.* 3 vols. Philadelphia: Lippincott, 1879.

Alexander, John K. *Render Them Submissive.* Amherst: University of Massachusetts Press, 1980.

Allen, James Sloan. *The Romance of Commerce and Culture: Capitalism, Modernism, and the Chicago-Aspen Crusade for Cultural Reform.* Chicago: University of Chicago Press, 1983.

Almond, Gabriel A., Marvin Chodorow, and Roy Harvey Pearce. "Progress and Its Discontents." *Bulletin of the American Academy of Arts and Science,* 35 (1981).

Appleby, Joyce. "Commercial Farming and the Agrarian Myth in the Early Republic." *Journal of American History,* 68 (1982).

Armstrong, John A. *The European Administrative Élite.* Princeton: Princeton University Press, 1973.

Banfield, Edward C., and James Q. Wilson. *City Politics.* Cambridge, Mass.: Harvard University Press, 1963.

Barnett, H. G. *Innovation: The Basis of Cultural Change*. New York: McGraw-Hill, 1953.

Bell, Daniel. *The Cultural Contradictions of Capitalism*. New York: Basic Books, 1976.

Bellah, R. N. "Civil Religion in America." *Daedalus* (v. 96 Winter 1967).

Bendix, Reinhard. *Work and Authority in Industry: Ideologies of Management in the Course of Industrialization*. New York: Wiley, 1956.

Boorstin, Daniel J. *The Americans*. 3 vols. New York: Random House, 1973.

———. *The Exploring Spirit*. New York: Random House, 1975.

Burns, Tom. *Industrial Man*. Baltimore: Penguin Books, 1969.

Brown, Gary Lawson. *Baltimore in the Nation, 1789–1861*. Chapel Hill: University of North Carolina Press, 1980.

Bryce, James. *The American Commonwealth*. 2 vols. New York: Macmillan, 1891.

Buford, C. H. "How to Become a Railroad President." *What's New* (November 1949).

Burlingame, Roger. *The American Coscience*. New York: Knopf, 1957.

Business Week Work Team. *The Reindustrialization of America*. New York: McGraw-Hill, 1982.

Calahan, Raymond E. *Education and the Cult of Efficiency*. Chicago: University of Chicago Press, 1962.

Campbell, Jeremy. *Grammatical Man: Information, Entropy, Language and Life*. New York: Simon & Schuster, 1982.

Carnegie, Andrew. *The Empire of Business*. New York: Doubleday, Page, 1902.

Chafe, William Henry. *The American Woman—Her Changing Social, Economic and Political Roles, 1920–1970*. New York: Oxford University Press, 1972.

Chandler, Alfred D. Jr. *Henry Vernon Poor: Business Editor, Analyst and Reformer*. Cambridge, Mass.: Harvard University Press, 1956.

———. "Henry Varnum Poor: Philosopher of Management." In William Miller, ed. *Men in Business*. Cambridge, Mass.: Harvard University Press, 1953.

———. *Strategy and Structure—Chapters in the History of Ameri-*

can Industrial Enterprise. Cambridge, Mass.: Harvard University Press, 1962.

————. *The Visible Hand: The Managerial Revolution in American Business.* Cambridge, Mass.: Harvard University Press, 1977.

————, and Steven Salsbury. *Pierre S. du Pont and the Making of the Modern Corporation.* New York: Harper & Row, 1972.

Chevalier, Michel. *Manners and Politics in the United States: A Series of Letters on North America.* Boston: Weeks, Jordan, and Company, 1939.

Clark, Victor S. *History of Manufactures in the United States 1607–1860.* Vol. 1. New York: McGraw-Hill, 1929.

Clement, Priscilla Ferguson. "The Philadelphia Welfare Crisis of the 1820s." *Pennsylvania Magazine of History and Biography,* 55 (April 1981).

Cochran, Thomas C. *Business in American Life, A History.* New York: McGraw-Hill, 1972.

————. "History and Cultural Crisis." *American Historical Review,* 78 (1973).

————. *The Inner Revolution.* New York: Torchbooks, 1964.

————. *Railroad Leaders 1845–1890: The Business Mind in Action.* Cambridge, Mass.: Harvard University Press, 1953.

————. "The Paradox of American Economic Growth." *Journal of American History,* 61 (March 1975).

————. *Social Change in America: The Twentieth Century.* New York: Harper & Row, 1972.

————. *The Pabst Brewing Company: A Business History.* New York: New York University Press, 1948.

————. *200 Years of American Business.* New York: Basic Books, 1977.

————. "The Sloan Report—American Culture and Business Management." *American Quarterly,* 27 (1975).

————. "The Social Scientists," in Robert E. Spiller and Eric Larabee, eds. *American Perspectives.* Cambridge, Mass.: Harvard University Press, 1961.

Coleman, Peter J. *Debtors and Creditors in America: Insolvency, Imprisonment for Debt, and Bankruptcy, 1807–1900.* Madison: State Historical Society, 1974.

Commager, Henry Steel. *The Empire of Reason.* New York: Oxford University Press, 1976.

Cooke, Jacob E. *Tench Cox and the Early Republic*. Chapel Hill: University of North Carolina Press, 1978.

Crafts, W. F. *Childhood: The Text-Book of the Age of Parents, Pastors and Teachers*. Boston: Lee and Shepard, 1875.

Cremin, Lawrence A. *The Transformation of the School*. New York: Knopf, 1961.

Croly, Herbert. *The Promise of America Life*. New York: Capricorn, 1964.

Crozier, Michael. *The Bureaucratic Phenomenon*. Chicago: University of Chicago Press, 1964.

Curti, Merle E., et al. *The Making of an American Community*. Stanford: Stanford University Press, 1959.

Davis, Joseph S. *Essays in the Early History of American Corporations*. Cambridge, Mass.: Harvard University Press, 1917.

Denison, Edward F. *Why Growth Rates Differ: Post War Experience in Nine Western Countries*. Washington, D.C.: Brookings, 1967.

Dewey, John. *Individualism Old and New*. New York: Putnam's, Capricorn, 1962.

Edwards, George W., and Herman G. Richey. *The School in the American Social Order*. Boston: Houghton Mifflin, 1947.

Feldman, Steve. "The Culture of Career Development." M.S. thesis. University of Pennsylvania, 1982.

Ferguson, Kathy. *Self, Society and Womankind, The Dialectic of Liberation*. Westport, CT., 1980.

Filler, Louis. ed. *Horace Mann on the Crisis in Education*. Yellow Springs, Ohio: Antioch Press, 1955.

Fogel, Robert W., and Stanley L. Engerman, eds. *The Reinterpretation of American Economic History*. New York: Harper & Row, 1971.

Freyer, T. A. *Forums of Order: Federal Courts and Business in American History*. Greenwich, Conn.: JAI Press, 1979.

Gallman, Robert E. "Gross National Product in the United States, 1834–1969." In National Bureau of Economic Research, *Conference on Income and Wealth*. No. 8. New York, 1946.

Garnett, Richard. ed. *Works of Charles Dickens*. Vol. 4. London, 1899.

Gates, Paul W. "The Homestead Act in an Incongruous Land System." *American Historical Review*, 40 (July 1936).

Geertz, Clifford. "The Way We Think Now, Toward an Ethnology of Modern Thought." *Bulletin of the American Academy of Arts and Science,* 35 (February 1982).

Gideon, Siegfried. *Mechanization Takes Command: A Contribution to History.* New York: Oxford University Press, 1948.

Gibb, George S. *The Whitesmiths of Taunton.* Cambridge, Mass.: Harvard University Press, 1944.

Gilfillan, S. C. *The Sociology of Invention.* Chicago: Follett, 1935.

Goldstein, Sidney, ed. *The Norristown Study.* Philadelphia: University of Pennsylvania Press, 1962.

Goodenough, Ward H. *Description and Comparison in Cultural Anthropology.* Chicago: Aldine, 1970.

Gordon, Suzanne. "The New Corporate Feminism." *The Nation,* February 5, 1983.

Graff, Harvey J. *The Literacy Myth: Literacy and Social Structure in the Nineteenth Century City.* New York: Academic Press, 1979.

Gutman, Herbert. "Work, Culture and Society in Industrial America, 1815–1919." *American Historical Review,* 78 (1973).

Hagnar, Charles V. *Early History of the Falls of the Schuylkill, Manayunk, Schuylkill and Lehigh Navigation Companies,* Philadelphia: Claxton, 1869.

Hamilton, Thomas. *Men and Manners in America.* Edinburgh: Blackwood, 1843.

Hancock, Harold. *The Industrial Worker Along the Brandywine, 1800–1830.* Wilmington: Hagley Report, August 1956.

Handlin, Oscar. ed. *John Dewey's Challenge to Education.* New York: Harper, 1959.

———, and Mary Hanellin. *Commonwealth: Massachusetts, 1734–1861.* New York: New York University Press, 1947.

Harvard University Program on Technology and Society. *Technology and Values.* Cambridge, Mass.: Harvard University Press, 1969.

Heidbreder, Edna. *Seven Psychologies.* New York: Century, 1933.

Henretta, James A. "Families and Forms—Mentalité in Pre-Industrial America." *William and Mary Quarterly,* 35 (January, 1978).

Henry, Jules. *Culture Against Man.* New York: Basic Books, 1973.

Herberg, Will. *Protestant, Catholic, Jew: An Essay in American Religious Sociology*. Garden City, N.Y.: Doubleday, 1955.

Heyerman, Christine Leigh. "The Fashion Among More Superior People: Charity and Social Change in Provincial New England, 1700–1740." *American Quarterly*, 34 (1982).

Hidy, Ralph W., and Muriel E. Hidy. *Pioneering in Big Business 1882–1911*. New York: Harper, 1955.

Hofstadter, Richard. *Anti-Intellectualism in American Life*. New York: Knopf, 1963.

Hudson, Winthrop S. *Religion in America*. 2d ed. New York: Scribner's, 1973.

Hughes, Thomas P. "A Technological Frontier." In Bruce Mazlish, ed., *The Railroad and the Space Program: An Exploration in Historical Analogy*. Cambridge, Mass.: The M.I.T. Press, 1965.

Hummel, Ralph. *The Bureaucratic Experience*. New York: St. Martin's, 1977.

Huntington, Samuel P. *American Politics: The Promise of Disharmony*. Cambridge, Mass.: The Belknap Press of Harvard University Press, 1981.

Hurst, Willard. *Law and Social Process in United States History*. Ann Arbor, Mich.: University of Michigan Law School, 1960.

Jeans, Sir James. *The Mysterious Universe*. New York: Macmillan, 1932.

Kammen, Michael. ed. *The Contrapuntal Civilization: Essays Toward a New Understanding of the American Experience*. New York: Crowell, 1971.

Kanter, Rosabeth Mass. *Men and Women of the Corporation*. New York: Basic Books, 1977.

Kendrick, John W. *Productivity Trends in the United States*. Princeton: Princeton University Press, 1961.

Korman, Gerd. *Industrialization, Immigrants and Americanizers: The View from Milwaukee, 1866–1921*. Madison: State Historical Society of Wisconsin, 1967.

Kroos, Herman E. *Executive Opinion: What Business Leaders Said and Thought on Economic Issues, 1920–1960*. Garden City, N.Y.: Doubleday, 1970.

Kuznets, Simon. *Modern Economic Growth: Rate, Structure and Spread*. Philadelphia: University of Pennsylvania Press, 1966.

————. "Notes on the Pattern of U.S. Economic Growth," in R. W. Fogel and S. L. Engerman, *The Reinterpretation of American Economic History.*

Langdon-Davies, John. *The New Age of Faith.* New York: Viking, 1925.

Lee, Everitt S. "The Turner Thesis Reexamined." *American Quarterly,* 13 (Spring 1961).

Leuchtenburg, William E. *The Perils of Prosperity.* Chicago: University of Chicago Press, 1958.

Litchfield, Paul W. *Industrial Voyage.* Garden City, N.Y.: Doubleday, 1954.

Littlefield, George E. *Early Schools and Schoolbooks of New England.* Cambridge: Cambridge University Press, 1964.

Lumsden, Charles J. and Edmund O. Wilson. *Promethean Fire: Reflections on the Origin of the Mind.* Cambridge, Mass.: Harvard University Press, 1983.

McConnell, Donald. *Economic Virtues in the United States: A History and an Interpretation.* New York: Arno, 1973.

Mandel, David. *Changing Art Changing Man.* New York: Horizon Press, 1967.

Marwedel, Emma. *Conscious Motherhood.* Boston: Heath, 1887.

Maurer, Herrymon. *Great Enterprise: Growth and Behavior of the Big Corporations.* New York: Macmillan, 1955.

May, Henry F. *The End of American Innocence.* New York: Knopf, 1959.

Mayo, Elton. *The Human Problems of an Industrial Civilization.* New York: Macmillan, 1933.

Meyers, Marvin. "Venturous Conservative" in Michael Kammen, ed. *The Contrapuntal Civilization.* New York: Crowell, 1971.

Michel, Jack. "In a Manner Suitable to their Degree. A Preliminary Investigation of the Material Culture of Early Pennsylvania." *Working Papers from the Regional Economic History Research Center,* Wilmington, 5:1 (1981).

Miller, Nathan. *The Enterprise of a Free People: Aspects of Economic Development in New York State During the Canal Period, 1792–1838.* Ithaca: Cornell University Press, 1962.

Miller, William, ed. *Men in Business: Essays in the History of Entrepreneurship.* Cambridge, Mass.: Harvard University Press, 1953.

Minnich Harvey C. *Old Favorites from the McGuffey Readers, 1836–1936.* New York: American Book, 1936.

Morison, Elting, ed. *The American Style: Essays on Value and Performance.* New York: Harper, 1958.

Murphey, Murray G. "An Approach to the Study of National Character." In Milford Spero, ed., *Meaning and Content in Cultural Anthropology.* New York: Free Press, 1965.

Neu, Irene D. *Erastus Corning, Merchant and Financier, 1794–1879.* Ithaca: Cornell University Press, 1960.

Noll, Mark A. "From the Great Awakening to the War of Independence: Christian Values in the American Revolution." *Christian Scholars Review,* 12 (1983).

Oakes, James. *A History of American Slave-holders.* New York: Knopf, 1982.

O'Shea, M. V. *First Steps in Child Training.* Chicago: Drake, 1920.

Parsons, Talcott. "Culture and Social Systems Revisited." In Louis Schneider and Charles Bonjean, eds. *The Idea of Culture in the Social Sciences.* Cambridge: Cambridge University Press, 1973.

Patterson, James T. *America's Struggle Against Poverty 1900–1980.* Cambridge, Mass.: Harvard University Press, 1981.

Perkins, Edwin J. *The Economy of Colonial America.* New York: Columbia University Press, 1980.

Pivar, David J. *Purity Crusade: Sexual Morality and Social Control, 1868–1900.* Westport, Conn.: Greenwood, 1973.

Potter, David. *People of Plenty: Economic Abundance and the American Character.* Chicago: University of Chicago Press, 1954.

Presthus, Robert V. *The Organizational Society: An Analysis and a Theory.* New York: Knopf, 1962.

Price, Jacob E. *France and the Chesapeake: A History of the French Tobacco Monopoly 1674–1791, and of its Relationship to the British and American Tobacco Trades.* 2 vols. Ann Arbor: University of Michigan Press, 1973.

Probst, Georg E. ed. *The Happy Republic: A Reader in Tocqueville's America.* New York: Torchbooks, 1962.

Riesman, David. *The Lonely Crowd.* New Haven: Yale University Press, 1950.

———. "The American Character in the Twentieth Century."

The Annals of the American Academy of Political and Social Science, March 1967.

Rodgers, Daniel T. *The Work Ethic in Industrial America 1850–1920.* Chicago: University of Chicago Press, 1978.

Rosenberg, Charles E. *No Other Gods: On Science and American Social Thought.* Baltimore: Johns Hopkins University Press, 1976.

Sargent, C. E. *Our Home or the Key to a Nobler Life.* Springfield, Mass.: King, 1884.

Schlesinger, Arthur M., Jr. "America: Experiment or Destiny?" *American Historical Review,* 81 (1976).

Schneider, Louis, and Charles Bonjean, eds. *The Idea of Culture in the Social Sciences.* Cambridge: Cambridge University Press, 1973.

Sharlin, Harold I., ed. *Business and Its Environment: Essays for Thomas C. Cochran.* Westport, Conn.: Greenwood, 1983.

————. *The Convergent Century: The Unification of Science in the Nineteenth Century.* New York: Abelard Schulman, 1966.

Sherwood, Mary E. *Amenities at Home.* New York: Appleton, 1882.

Smith, Billy G. "The Best Poor Man's Country: Living Standards of the Lower Sort in Late 18th Century Philadelphia." *Working Papers from the Regional Economic History Research Center,* Wilmington, Vol. 2, No. 4 (1979).

Spiller, Robert E. and Erich Larrabee, eds. *The National Self-Image in the Twentieth Century, American Perspectives.* Cambridge, Mass.: Harvard University Press, 1961.

Staley, Eugene, ed. *Creating an Industrial Civilization.* New York: Harper, 1952.

Steere, Geoffrey H. "Changing Values in Child Socialization: A Study of U.S. Child-Rearing Literature, 1865–1929." Ph.D. dissertation, University of Pennsylvania, 1964.

Strassman, W. Paul. *Risk and Technological Innovation: American Manufacturing During the Nineteenth Century.* Ithaca: Cornell University Press, 1959.

Sweet, William W. *Revivalism in America: Its Origin, Growth, and Decline.* Gloucester, Mass.: P. Smith, 1965.

Taylor, Frederick Winslow. *The Principles of Scientific Management.* New York: Harper, 1911.

Tocqueville, Alexis de. *Democracy in America.* 2 vols. New York: Century, 1898.

U.S. Bureau of the Census. *Historical Statistics of the United States Colonial Times to 1957.* Washington, D.C.: Government Printing Office, 1960.

Wallace, Anthony, F. C. *Culture and Personality.* New York: Random House, 1961.

———. *Rockdale: The Growth of an American Village in the Early Industrial Revolution.* New York: Knopf, 1978.

Watson, John B. "Psychology as the Behaviorist Views It." *Psychological Review,* 20 (1913).

———. *Psychology from the Standpoint of a Behaviorist.* Philadelphia: Lippincott, 1919.

Weiss, Johannes. *Earliest Christianity: A History of the Period A.D. 30–150.* 2 vols. New York: Harper Torchbooks, 1963.

West, Mary Allen. *Childhood: Its Care and Culture.* Chicago: Law, King, Law, 1888.

White, Morton. *Pragmatism and the American Mind: Essays and Reviews in Philosophy and Intellectual History.* New York: Oxford University Press, 1973.

Whyte, William H., Jr. *The Organization Man.* New York: Simon & Schuster, 1956.

Williams, Robin M. "Individual and Group Values." *The Annals of the American Academy of Political and Social Science,* 37 (May 1967).

Williamson, Jeffrey G. "Late Nineteenth Century Retardation: A Neoclassical Analusis." *Journal of Economic History,* 33 (September 1973).

Winnpenny, Thomas R. "Cultural Factors in the Persistence of Hand Technology in Lancaster, Pennsylvania." *Pennsylvania History,* 50 (1983).

Woodward, J. "Management Systems" in Tom Burns, *Industrial Man.* Baltimore: Penguin, 1969.

Wright, Julia McNair. *Practical Life or Ways and Means for Developing Character and Resources.* Philadelphia: McCurdy, 1881.

Wright, J. Patrick. *On a Clear Day You Can See General Motors: John Z. Delorean's Look Inside the Automotive Giant.* New York: Avon, 1979.

Zuckerman, Michael. "Fate, Flux, and Good Fellowship: An Early Virginia Design for the Dilemma of American Business" in Harold Sharlin, ed. *Business and Its Environment: Essays for Thomas C. Cochran*. Westport, Conn.: Greenwood, 1983.

Index